EYEWITNESS PROJECT BOOKS
HUMAN BODY

by Claire Watts

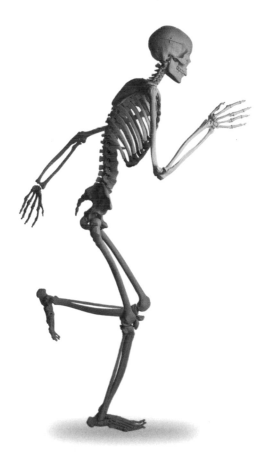

LONDON, NEW YORK,
MELBOURNE, MUNICH, AND DELHI

Educational Consultants Linda B. Gambrell
and Geraldine Taylor

Project Editor Susan Malyan
Art Editor Peter Radcliffe
Senior Editor Jane Yorke
Senior Art Editor Owen Peyton Jones
Managing Editor Camilla Hallinan
Managing Art Editor Martin Wilson
Publishing Manager Sunita Gahir
Category Publisher Andrea Pinnington
DK Picture Library Claire Bowers, Rose Horridge
Production Controller Lucy Baker
DTP Designers Siu Chan, Andy Hilliard, Ronaldo Julien
Jacket Designer Neal Cobourne

First published in the United States in 2007 as
Eyewitness Workbooks Human Body
This edition published in Great Britain in 2008 by
Dorling Kindersley Limited,
80 Strand, London WC2R 0RL

2 4 6 8 10 9 7 5 3 1
ED597 – 06/08

A CIP catalogue record for this book
is available from the British Library.

ISBN: 978-1-40532-168-6

Colour reproduction by Media Development Printing Limited, UK
Printed and bound by L.Rex Printing Co. Ltd, China

Discover more at
www.dk.com

Contents

Fast facts

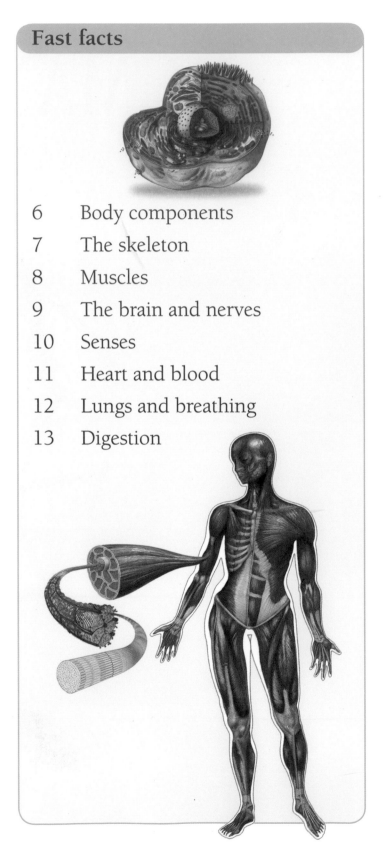

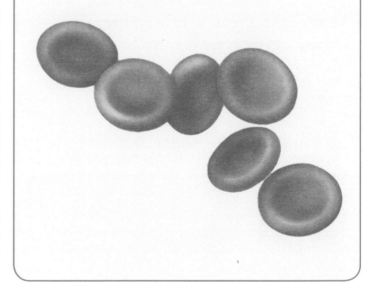

How this book can help your child

Eyewitness Project Books offer a fun and colourful range of stimulating titles in the subjects of history, science, and geography. Specially designed to appeal to children of 8 years and up, each project book aims to:

- develop a child's knowledge of a popular topic
- provide practice of key skills and reinforce classroom learning
- nurture a child's special interest in a subject.

The series is devised and written with the expert advice of educational and reading consultants, and supports the school curriculum.

About this book

Eyewitness Project Book Human Body is an activity-packed exploration of how our bodies work. Inside you will find:

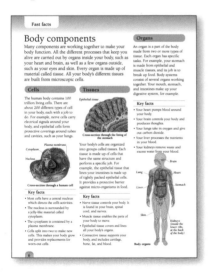

Fast facts

This section presents key information as concise facts, which are easy to digest, learn, and remember. Encourage your child to start by reading through the valuable information in the Fast facts section and studying the statistics chart inside the flap at the back of the book before trying out the activities.

Activities

The enjoyable, fill-in activities are designed to develop information recall and help your child practise cross-referencing skills. Each activity can be completed using information provided on the page, in the Fast facts section, or on the back-cover chart. Your child should work systematically through the book and tackle just one or two activity topics in a session. Encourage your child by checking answers together and offering extra guidance when necessary.

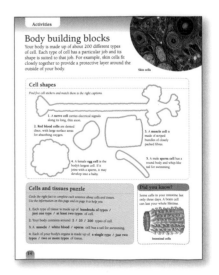

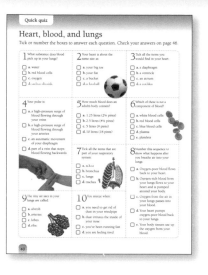

Quick quiz

There are six pages of multiple-choice questions to test your child's new-found knowledge of the subject. Children should only try answering the quiz questions once all of the activity section has been completed. As your child finishes each page of themed questions, check the answers together.

Answers and Progress chart

All the answers are supplied in full at the back of the book, so no prior knowledge of the subject is required.

Use the Progress chart to motivate your child and be positive about his or her achievements. On the completion of each activity or quiz topic, reward good work with a gold star.

Certificate

There is a Certificate of excellence at the back of the book for your child to fill in, remove, and display on the wall.

Lift the flap

The chart inside the back cover is a fun learning tool, packed with fascinating facts and figures about the body. Happy learning!

Important information

- For the taste test on page 31, avoid foods to which the taster may be allergic. All other activities in this book can be carried out without adult supervision, although the activity on page 28 needs an adult to take part.

- Encourage your child to conduct their own simple investigations.

They could look at their own skin with a magnifying glass, for example.

- If your child shows a particular interest in one of the topics, try extending some of the activities. For example, your child could keep a food diary of all the food he or she eats, then see if it fits with the food pyramid on page 30.

Body components

Many components are working together to make your body function. All the different processes that keep you alive are carried out by organs inside your body, such as your heart and brain, as well as a few organs outside, such as your eyes and skin. Every organ is made up of material called tissue. All your body's different tissues are built from microscopic cells.

Cells

The human body contains 100 trillion living cells. There are about 200 different types of cell in your body, each with a job to do. For example, nerve cells carry electrical signals around your body, and epithelial cells form protective coverings around tubes and cavities, such as your lungs.

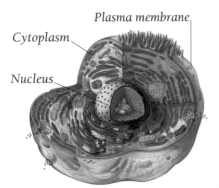

Cytoplasm
Plasma membrane
Nucleus

Cross-section through a human cell

Key facts

- Most cells have a central nucleus which directs the cell's activities.
- The nucleus is surrounded by a jelly-like material called cytoplasm.
- The cytoplasm is contained by a plasma membrane.
- Cells split into two to make new cells. This makes your body grow and provides replacements for worn-out cells.

Tissues

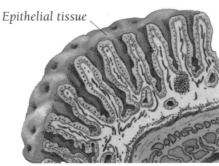

Epithelial tissue

Cross-section through the lining of the stomach

Your body's cells are organized into groups called tissues. Each tissue is made up of cells that have the same structure and perform a specific job. For example, the epithelial tissue that lines your intestines is made up of tightly packed epithelial cells. It provides a protective barrier against micro-organisms in food.

Key facts

- Nerve tissue controls your body. It is found in your brain, spinal cord, and nerves.
- Muscle tissue enables the parts of your body to move.
- Epithelial tissue covers and lines all your body's organs.
- Connective tissue supports your body, and includes cartilage, bone, fat, and blood.

Organs

An organ is a part of the body made from two or more types of tissue. Each organ has specific tasks. For example, your stomach is made from epithelial and muscle tissues, and its job is to break up food. Body systems consist of several organs working together. Your mouth, stomach, and intestines make up your digestive system, for example.

Key facts

- Your heart pumps blood around your body.
- Your brain controls your body and produces thoughts.
- Your lungs take in oxygen and give out carbon dioxide.
- Your liver processes the nutrients in your blood.
- Your kidneys remove waste and excess water from your blood.

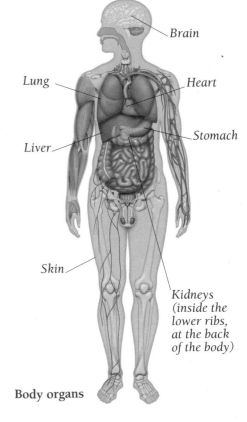

Brain
Lung
Heart
Liver
Stomach
Skin
Kidneys (inside the lower ribs, at the back of the body)

Body organs

The skeleton

Your body is supported by a strong framework of bones, called your skeleton. These bones also protect your soft inner tissues and organs. Bones are hard and inflexible, but they can move at the points where they meet, called joints. Bones vary in size and shape, depending on their purpose, from the massive weight-bearing bones in your legs, to the tiny ear bones that help you to detect sound.

Skeletal system

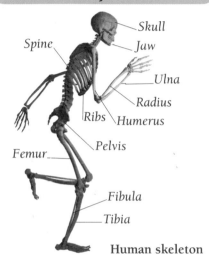

Human skeleton

Skull
Jaw
Spine
Ulna
Radius
Humerus
Ribs
Pelvis
Femur
Fibula
Tibia

There are 206 bones in an adult's body. Each bone links with others to form the skeletal system, or skeleton. Your spine runs from the base of your skull to the base of your pelvis. All your other bones are arranged symmetrically on either side of your body.

Key facts

- The spine, skull, and ribcage make up the axial skeleton. Its main function is to protect organs.
- The arms, shoulders, legs, and pelvis form the appendicular skeleton. These bones mainly allow the body to move.
- The shoulder blades and hips link the appendicular skeleton to the spine.

Bones

The strongest part of a bone is the hard, outer layer, which is called compact bone. Inside a bone is a soft, fatty tissue called marrow. The ends of bones are filled with air pockets, to make them strong but light. Tough cords, called tendons, attach bones to the muscles that control their movement.

Key facts

- Bones are made from living tissue, and, like other tissues, their cells are continually breaking down and renewing themselves.
- The marrow in certain bones produces new blood cells.
- Bones store the mineral calcium which is used to make your nerves and muscles function.

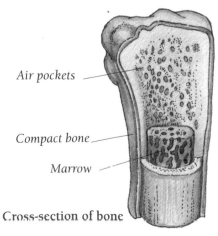

Air pockets
Compact bone
Marrow

Cross-section of bone

Joints

Your bones meet at joints. At a joint, the bone's surface is covered with slippery cartilage and lubricated with synovial fluid which help it to move smoothly. Most joints are held together with bands called ligaments. Some joints, such as your knees, allow movement in just one direction. Other joints, such as your shoulders, allow many different movements.

Types of joints

Hinge joint, such as knee

Ball and socket joint, such as shoulder

Pivot joint, such as skull on spine

Ellipsoidal joint, such as wrist

Key facts

- Joints with the smallest variety of movement, such as your knees, are the strongest.
- Joints with a large variety of movement, such as your shoulders, are much weaker and may dislocate or slip.
- The bones of your skull meet at fixed joints, which allow no movement at all.

Muscles

Beneath your skin, your body's flesh is made up of layers of strong, fibrous tissue, called muscle. Every movement your body makes depends on muscles, from automatic movements, such as breathing, to movements you control consciously, such as chewing. Muscle movements are triggered by electrical impulses from your brain.

Muscles

Your muscles are made of thick bundles of overlapping fibres. Each fibre contains tiny parallel strands, called myofibrils. Nerve signals make the myofibrils contract, so that the muscle fibres become shorter and tighter. This produces a pulling force which moves the bone or organ that the muscle is attached to.

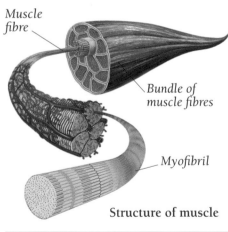

Muscle fibre

Bundle of muscle fibres

Myofibril

Structure of muscle

Key facts

- Skeletal muscles make movements which are consciously controlled by your brain, such as walking.
- Smooth muscles perform your body's automatic functions, such as pushing food along your digestive system.
- Throughout your life, cardiac (heart) muscle contracts every fraction of a second to keep your heart beating.

Skeletal muscles

Most of the muscles in your body are skeletal muscles. These muscles have long fibres that can contract quickly and powerfully. Some skeletal muscles are tiny, such as the muscles that move your eyeballs. Others are huge, such as the triangular deltoid muscle that moves your shoulder.

Key facts

- There are more than 600 skeletal muscles in your body. They make up 40 per cent of your weight.
- The layer of muscles just below your skin is called surface or superficial muscle. Muscles below this are called deep muscles.

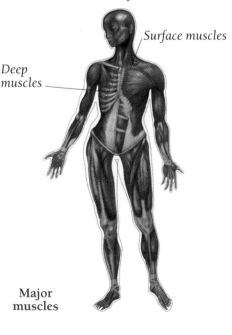

Surface muscles

Deep muscles

Major muscles

Movement

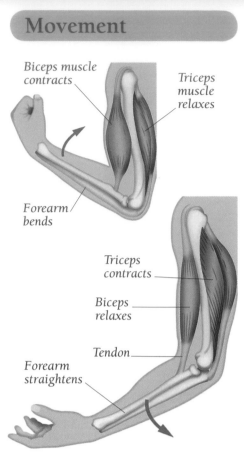

Biceps muscle contracts

Triceps muscle relaxes

Forearm bends

Triceps contracts

Biceps relaxes

Tendon

Forearm straightens

Bending and straightening the arm

Most skeletal muscles are attached to two or more bones. They stretch from one bone to the other across a joint. When a muscle contracts, it pulls on the bones it is attached to, creating movement. Most muscles work in pairs, with one muscle in the pair contracting while the other one relaxes.

Key facts

- Skeletal muscles are attached to bones by tough cords, called tendons.
- When your body is not moving, all your muscles are partially contracted, to hold your body in position.
- Muscles cannot push. They can only pull bones towards or away from each other.

The brain and nerves

Your nervous system is in control of almost everything that happens in your body. It is made up of your brain, spinal cord, and nerves that link to every part of your body. This vast network is constantly detecting what is happening in and around your body and issuing instructions about how to react.

Nervous system

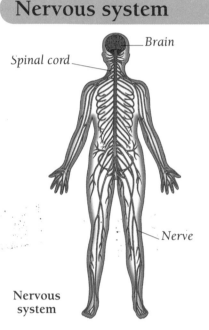

Brain

Spinal cord

Nerve

Nervous system

Your brain and spinal cord are known as the central nervous system. These organs receive information from the nerves around your body. They analyse the information, and send out instructions along other nerves if necessary. For example, if you prick a finger, they send an order to move your hand away.

Key facts

- Your spinal cord is a bundle of nerves that runs down from your brain inside your spine.
- Involuntary activities that you do not think about, such as breathing, are controlled by both your brain and your spinal cord.

Brain

The largest part of your brain, the cerebrum, has a heavily folded surface divided into two halves. It overhangs the other main parts of your brain, the cerebellum and the brainstem. The cerebrum's outer layer, called the grey matter, is made of nerve cells. It controls complex brain functions, such as thought. The inner layer, called the white matter, is made of nerve fibres, which transmit electrical impulses.

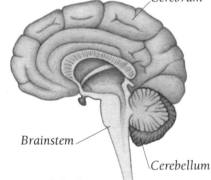

Cerebrum

Brainstem

Cerebellum

Structure of the brain

Key facts

- The brainstem controls digestion, breathing, and the heart beat.
- The cerebellum controls muscle coordination.
- Conscious thinking takes place in the cerebrum. This includes memory, learning, speech, and conscious control of your body's movements.

Nerves

A nerve cell, or neuron, has a cell body, with fine branches called dendrites, and a long projecting fibre called the axon. Nerves are made up of bundles of axons. Signals pass along the axons to the nerve endings as impulses of electricity, moving at more than 400 kph (250 mph). The signals then leap across the gaps to the dendrites of the next neurons.

Key facts

- The 12 pairs of nerves that branch from your brain are called the cranial nerves.
- The 31 pairs that branch from your spinal cord are called the spinal nerves.
- Sensory neurons send messages triggered by different sensations to your central nervous system.
- Motor neurons carry signals from your central nervous system to muscles to make them contract.
- Association neurons transfer signals between other neurons.

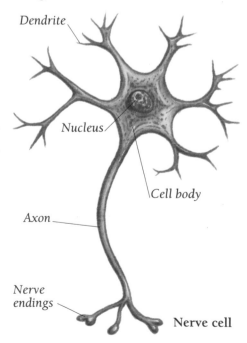

Dendrite

Nucleus

Cell body

Axon

Nerve endings

Nerve cell

Senses

You have five senses: sight, hearing, taste, smell, and touch. They tell your brain what is happening around your body. Your five sets of sense organs – eyes, ears, tongue, nose, and skin – are packed with specialized neurons that detect things in the outside world, such as light or sound. They convert this information into nerve signals, which travel to your brain.

Sight

Your eyes are round bags of clear jelly-like fluid surrounded by a tough white coating, called the sclera. The retina at the back of your eye is covered with billions of cells, called rods and cones. These react when light hits them. Rods see in black and white, and cones see in colour.

Key facts

- Light rays enter your eye through the pupil.
- Light is focused on to your retina by the cornea and lens.
- Light-sensitive cells on the retina pick up the image of what you are seeing and send it along the optic nerve to your brain.

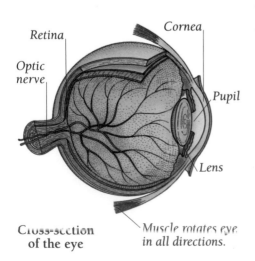

Cross-section of the eye

Retina

Optic nerve

Cornea

Pupil

Lens

Muscle rotates eye in all directions.

Hearing

Sound is made up of a stream of vibrations. Your ears collect these and convert them to electrical signals which are passed to your brain. Most of your ear is inside your skull. The only part that can be seen outside your body is the pinna, or ear flap.

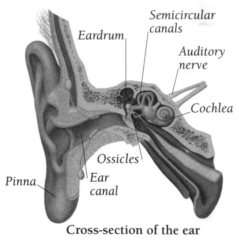

Semicircular canals

Eardrum

Auditory nerve

Cochlea

Ossicles

Pinna

Ear canal

Cross-section of the ear

Key facts

- The pinna directs sound into the ear canal.
- Sound waves bounce off the eardrum, making it vibrate.
- Tiny bones called ossicles magnify the vibrations and send them to the cochlea.
- Fluid inside the cochlea vibrates, moving millions of tiny hairs which send nerve signals along the auditory nerve to your brain.

Taste and smell

Your sense of taste detects chemicals in saliva, while smell detects chemicals in the air. Smell works well on its own, but taste cannot work without smell.

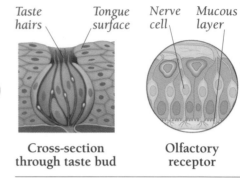

Taste hairs　*Tongue surface*　*Nerve cell*　*Mucous layer*

Cross-section through taste bud　　**Olfactory receptor**

Key facts

- Most tastes are detected by taste buds on your tongue, but some taste detectors are scattered around your mouth.
- Olfactory receptors behind the bridge of your nose detect smell.

Touch

The sense of touch is detected by sensors all over your body. It allows you to find out the shape, size, temperature, and texture of things, and to feel pain.

Key facts

- Some body parts, such as your fingers and tongue, have more touch sensors than others, making them highly sensitive.
- Specialized nerve endings in your skin detect different sensations.

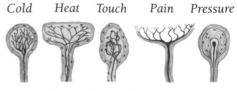

Cold　*Heat*　*Touch*　*Pain*　*Pressure*

Nerve endings in the skin

Heart and blood

Blood flows around your body in a continuous circuit, through a network of vessels thousands of kilometres long. It supplies every tissue in your body with oxygen and nutrients and carries away waste. This circulatory system is powered by your heart, an organ the size of a clenched fist, which acts as a pump.

Blood

The colour of your blood comes from the millions of round red blood cells in it. These float in a watery fluid, called plasma, along with white blood cells and platelets. Your blood transports oxygen, nutrients, and waste. It also fights infection and regulates your temperature by distributing heat evenly around your body.

Key facts

- Red blood cells store oxygen and release it around your body.
- White blood cells detect and destroy micro-organisms that cause disease.
- Platelets stop leaks from blood vessels by making blood clot.
- Plasma carries nutrients and hormones around your body.
- Blood is a connective tissue, like bone and cartilage, but it is liquid rather than solid.

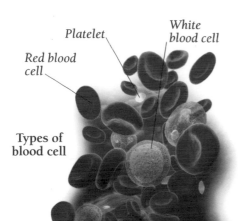

Types of blood cell

Platelet
White blood cell
Red blood cell

Heart

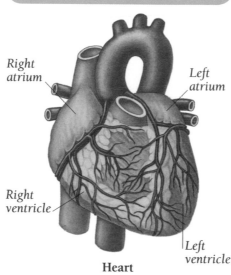

Right atrium
Left atrium
Right ventricle
Left ventricle

Heart

Your heart is a muscular pump which sits between your lungs, tilted slightly to the left side. It contracts once every four-fifths of a second, to pump blood around your body. With each contraction, valves close to stop the blood flowing backwards. This produces the thudding sound of your heart beat.

Key facts

- Your heart has two upper chambers, the atria, and two lower chambers, the ventricles.
- Blood flows into the atria. When they are full, they pump blood into the ventricles below.
- The ventricles pump blood to the lungs and around your body.

Circulatory system

Blood flowing through your lungs picks up oxygen. It travels to your heart, which pumps it around your body. As the blood moves along the blood vessels, it releases oxygen into the surrounding cells and picks up waste carbon dioxide. Oxygen-poor blood returns to your heart, which pumps it back to your lungs to pick up more oxygen.

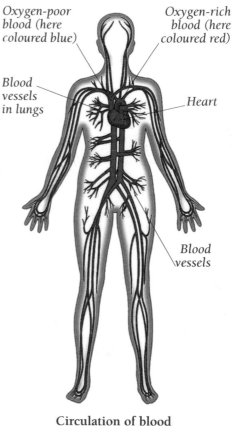

Oxygen-poor blood (here coloured blue)
Oxygen-rich blood (here coloured red)
Blood vessels in lungs
Heart
Blood vessels

Circulation of blood

Key facts

- Vessels called arteries carry oxygen-rich blood from the heart and lungs to your body.
- Vessels called veins carry oxygen-poor blood from your body back to the heart and lungs.
- It takes about one minute for all of your blood to pass through your lungs and around your body.

Lungs and breathing

You breathe in 20,000 times a day, drawing air into your lungs. The organs you use to breathe make up your respiratory system. They extract oxygen from the air and send it around your body in the blood. Every cell in your body uses oxygen to release energy from the food you eat, so all cells need a constant supply of oxygen.

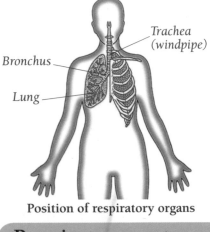

Position of respiratory organs

Trachea (windpipe)
Bronchus
Lung

Respiratory system

Each time you breathe in, air enters your body through your nose and mouth, and moves down your trachea into your lungs. There, oxygen from the air is absorbed into the bloodstream, ready to be transported around your body. Waste carbon dioxide passes from your blood into your lungs and leaves your body each time you breathe out.

Key facts

- As air passes through your nose, it is warmed and moistened, and harmful particles are filtered out.
- A flap of cartilage, called the epiglottis, stops food and drink entering your trachea.
- Your trachea divides into two large airways called the bronchi. Each one, called a bronchus, enters one of your lungs.

Lungs

You have two pink, spongy lungs inside your chest cavity. Inside your lungs, the two bronchi branch into tiny airways, called bronchioles. At the end of each bronchiole is a tiny air sac, called an alveolus. Oxygen passes through the walls of the alveoli into blood vessels that surround them, and carbon dioxide passes back into the alveoli.

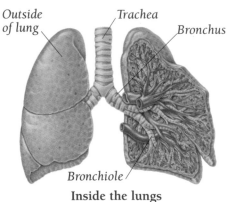

Outside of lung
Trachea
Bronchus
Bronchiole
Inside the lungs

Key facts

- Your right lung has three sections, called lobes. Your left lung has only two, to make room for your heart on this side of your body.
- Every minute, about 5–6 litres (9–10 pints) of air pass through your lungs.
- Each lung contains millions of alveoli, which look like bunches of grapes at the ends of the bronchioles.

Breathing

When you breathe, your lungs expand and shrink in a rhythmic action. This draws air in and pushes it out. Adults breathe in and out about 12–15 times per minute, taking in around 0.5 litres (1 pint) of air with each breath.

Key facts

- Breathing is caused by movements of your ribs and diaphragm, a sheet of muscle which lies below your ribcage.

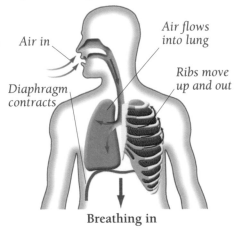

Air in
Air flows into lung
Ribs move up and out
Diaphragm contracts
Breathing in

- To draw air into your lungs, your diaphragm pushes down and your ribs move up and out, increasing the space in your chest cavity.

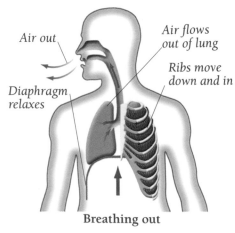

Air out
Air flows out of lung
Ribs move down and in
Diaphragm relaxes
Breathing out

- To push air out of your lungs, your diaphragm relaxes upwards and your ribs relax downwards, decreasing the space in your chest.

Digestion

Your body needs food to build and repair itself, and to provide energy for all its processes. Before your body can make use of the food you eat, it has to be broken down into small particles, called nutrients, which can be absorbed into your blood. The process of breaking down and absorbing food is called digestion.

Digestive system

The main organ of your digestive system is a long muscular tube, called the digestive tract. This is divided into four parts: the oesophagus, the stomach, and the small and large intestines. Your pancreas, gall bladder, and liver also play a part in digestion.

Key facts

- Digestion begins in your mouth, where your teeth break food into smaller pieces.
- Fluid called saliva softens food so it can slide down your throat.
- Your tongue shapes food into a ball and pushes it to the back of your throat, where you swallow it.
- Food enters your oesophagus and moves down into your stomach.

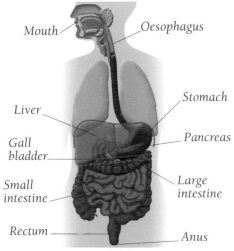

Organs of the digestive system

Stomach

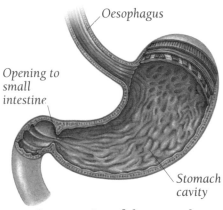

Cross-section of the stomach

Inside your stomach, food is churned around by muscle contractions in the stomach wall. The lining of your stomach secretes acid and other chemicals that gradually break down the food, turning it into a soupy liquid called chyme. This liquid is released in spurts into your small intestine.

Key facts

- It takes about 10 seconds for food to travel down your oesophagus to your stomach.
- Food stays in your stomach for about four hours.
- Stomach acid is so powerful that it can dissolve metal.
- A layer of mucus lining your stomach prevents stomach acid from digesting your stomach wall.

Intestines

Your small intestine is lined with millions of tiny projections called villi, packed with blood vessels. Nutrients from the chyme pass through the walls of the villi into the blood. By the time the chyme reaches your large intestine, it is made up largely of waste and water. The water is absorbed into the bloodstream and the waste is formed into faeces in the rectum.

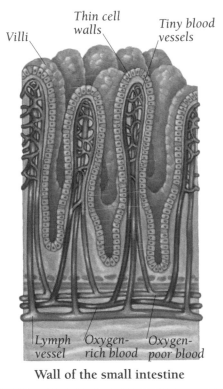

Wall of the small intestine

Key facts

- Your small intestine is about 5 m (17 ft) long.
- Your large intestine is only 1.5 m (5 ft) long, but it is wider than your small intestine.
- Food can remain in your small intestine for up to five hours.
- Food spends up to 36 hours in your large intestine.
- Faeces reach your rectum between 20 and 45 hours after you swallowed the food.

Body building blocks

Your body is made up of about 200 different types of cell. Each type of cell has a particular job and its shape is suited to that job. For example, skin cells fit closely together to provide a protective layer around the outside of your body.

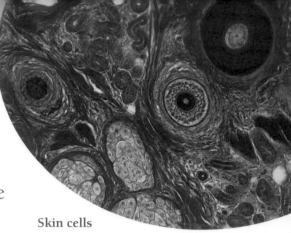

Skin cells

Cell shapes

Find five cell stickers and match them to the right captions.

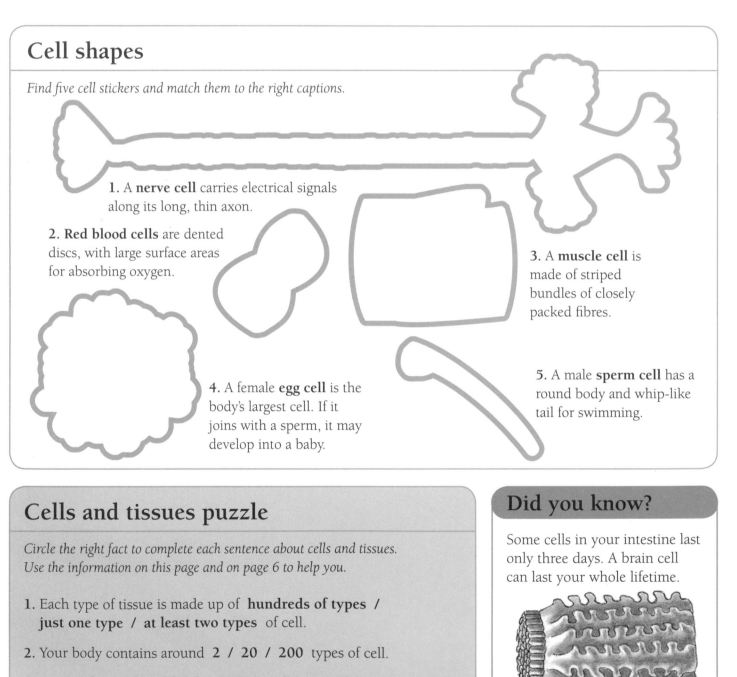

1. A **nerve cell** carries electrical signals along its long, thin axon.

2. Red blood cells are dented discs, with large surface areas for absorbing oxygen.

3. A **muscle cell** is made of striped bundles of closely packed fibres.

4. A female **egg cell** is the body's largest cell. If it joins with a sperm, it may develop into a baby.

5. A male **sperm cell** has a round body and whip-like tail for swimming.

Cells and tissues puzzle

Circle the right fact to complete each sentence about cells and tissues. Use the information on this page and on page 6 to help you.

1. Each type of tissue is made up of **hundreds of types / just one type / at least two types** of cell.

2. Your body contains around **2 / 20 / 200** types of cell.

3. A **muscle / white blood / sperm** cell has a tail for swimming.

4. Each of your body's organs is made up of **a single type / just two types / two or more types** of tissue.

Did you know?

Some cells in your intestine last only three days. A brain cell can last your whole lifetime.

Intestinal cells

Body systems

A group of organs and tissues that work together to perform a task, such as digesting food or moving the body, is called a system. Each system depends on other systems to work. For example, the muscular system moves the bones that make up the skeletal system.

Guess the system

Can you name these body systems? Look at the picture labels and use the information in the system definitions on the right and on the back-cover chart to help you. Choose from:

**nervous   circulatory   muscular
digestive   respiratory   skeletal**

System definitions

Nervous system: carries messages round the body
Main components: nerves, brain, spinal cord

Muscular system: moves the body
Main components: muscles

Circulatory system: moves blood around the body
Main components: heart, blood vessels

Respiratory system: supplies the body with oxygen
Main components: lungs

Digestive system: processes food
Main components: stomach, intestines

Skeletal system: supports the body
Main components: bones

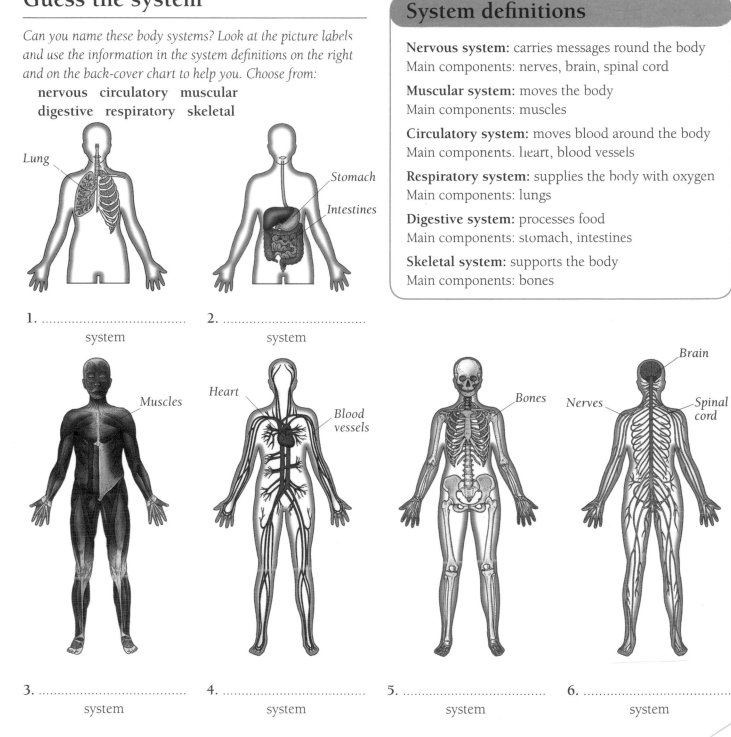

Lung

Stomach

Intestines

1. .... system

2. .... system

Muscles

Heart

Blood vessels

Bones

Brain

Nerves

Spinal cord

3. .... system

4. .... system

5. .... system

6. .... system

1

Big bones, small bones

The 206 bones that make up your skeleton are divided into five different groups, depending on their shape. Your bones are joined together at more than 400 flexible joints, which allow you to move in lots of different ways, from nodding your head to doing a somersault.

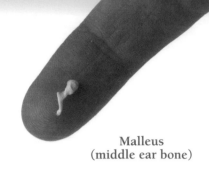

Malleus
(middle ear bone)

Skeleton jigsaw

Find five bone stickers to complete this skeleton. Then draw lines to link the labels to the right bones. Use the information on page 7 if you need help.

Skull

Spine

Collar bone

Ribs

Radius
and ulna

Humerus

Femur

Pelvis

Tibia and
fibula

Sorting bones

Can you work out which group each of these bones fits into? Write a number in each of the boxes to match the types of bone listed below.

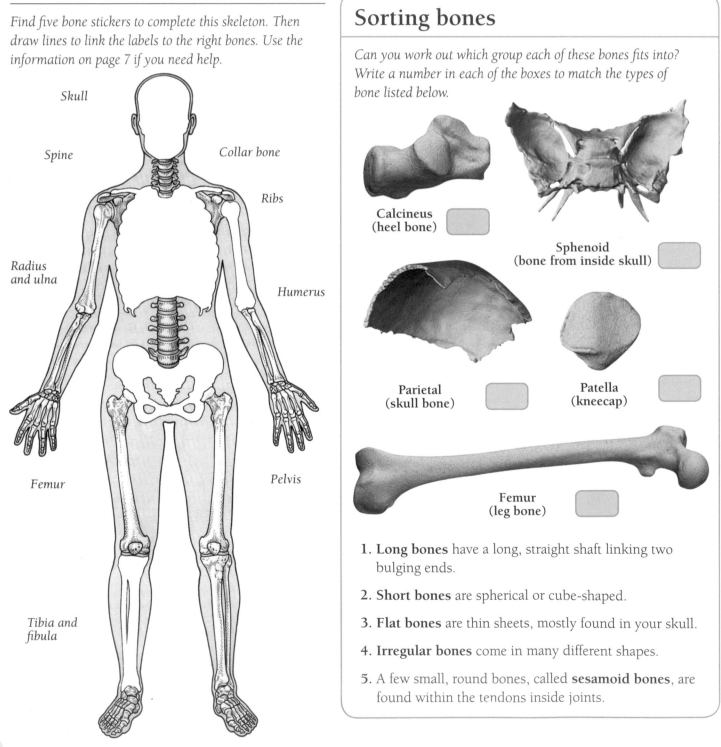

Calcineus
(heel bone)

Sphenoid
(bone from inside skull)

Parietal
(skull bone)

Patella
(kneecap)

Femur
(leg bone)

1. **Long bones** have a long, straight shaft linking two bulging ends.

2. **Short bones** are spherical or cube-shaped.

3. **Flat bones** are thin sheets, mostly found in your skull.

4. **Irregular bones** come in many different shapes.

5. A few small, round bones, called **sesamoid bones**, are found within the tendons inside joints.

Did you know?

In an adult, it takes just six weeks to mend a broken long bone, such as a leg bone. Children's long bones can repair themselves even more quickly.

Bone facts

• When a foetus (a baby in the womb) first develops a skeleton, it is not made of bone, but of tough, flexible tissue called cartilage.

• Some of the cartilage solidifies into bone before the baby is born. A newborn baby has over 300 separate bones, with lots of cartilage in between.

• By the age of 20, most bones have solidified. The adult skeleton now contains just 206 bones, and has stopped growing.

• Cells inside the bones continue to make new bone to replace parts that are worn out.

• Bone tissue is replaced much more slowly in elderly people, which makes their bones more fragile. By the age of 70, a person's bones can be a third lighter than they were at 40.

Joint puzzle

Complete the sentences under each picture, using a joint and a body part from the lists below. Use the information on page 7 to help you. Choose from:

JOINTS	BODY PARTS
ellipsoidal	head
ball and socket	shoulder
hinge	wrist
pivot	knee

1. A swimmer uses the ....joint in his ....to raise his arm while doing the crawl.

2. A golfer bends the .... joint in his .... to move his hand and swing his club.

3. A footballer uses the .... joint in his .... to bend his leg and kick the ball.

4. A ballet dancer keeps her head facing forward at all times, by turning her .... on a .... joint.

True or false?

Read the following sentences about bones. Using the information on this page and on page 7, tick the boxes to show which facts are true and which are false.

	TRUE	FALSE
1. A newborn baby has more than 300 separate bones.	☐	☐
2. Old people's bones are lighter than younger people's.	☐	☐
3. The ends of bones are filled with air pockets.	☐	☐
4. The skeleton stops growing by the age of 18 months.	☐	☐

Moving muscles

Your muscles need oxygen to help them move. The harder they work, the more oxygen they need. When skeletal muscles move, they normally use sudden bursts of power, which use up a lot of oxygen, so they tire easily. If your blood can't carry oxygen to your active muscles quickly enough, your muscles start to ache.

Clench test

Try this clench test to find out why muscles ache.

1 Hold your hand above your head and clench and unclench your fist. How many times can you clench it before it starts feeling uncomfortable? ....

2 Now try it with your other hand, but this time hold it down by your side. How many times can you clench before this feels uncomfortable? ....

Turn to page 44 to find out what your results mean.

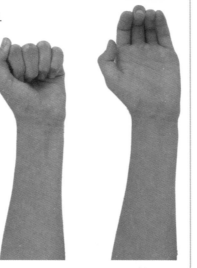

Relax test

Try this experiment to see your muscles in action.

1 Clasp your hands together with the fingers interlocked.

2 Stretch out your forefingers straight and parallel to each other, but not touching. What happens to your forefingers when you let your muscles relax?

....

Turn to page 44 to find out what your results mean.

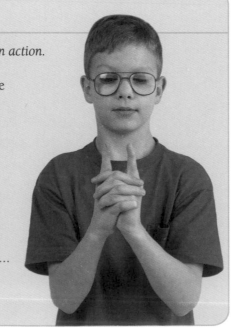

Muscle types

These boxes each contain facts about one type of muscle. Can you name each type from the list below, using the information on page 8 to help you? Choose from:

skeletal   cardiac   smooth

1. ....muscle
- It makes the heart beat.
- It is automatically controlled.
- It contracts and relaxes constantly.
- It never tires.

2. ....muscle
- It can be consciously controlled by the brain.
- It contracts in short bursts.
- It remains slightly contracted when at rest.
- It tires easily.

3. ....muscle
- It performs the body's automatic functions, such as breathing.
- It contracts slowly.
- It can stay contracted for long periods.
- It does not tire easily.

Did you know?

A muscle fibre is thinner than a hair, and can be up to 30 cm (1 ft) long.

Muscle fibre

Fit and healthy

Exercise is vital for keeping your body fit and healthy. When you are fit, all your body's systems are able to work properly. Exercise improves the strength and suppleness of your body, and improves the efficiency of your heart and lungs. It also helps you to maintain a healthy weight.

Exercise chart

Experts say that school-age children should do 60 minutes of physical activity every day. Keep an exercise log for a week, to find out how active you are.

1 For each part of each day, fill in what activity you have done and how long you spent doing it. Include all kinds of physical exercise you do on your chart, such as: walking to school, walking the dog, playing football, swimming, or even vacuuming your bedroom.

2 At the end of the day, add up the total amount of time you have spent exercising. If you have not managed 60 minutes that day, think about how you could improve your total the next day. For instance, you could get a friend to practise a sport with you.

	Monday	Tuesday	Wednesday	Thursday	Friday	Saturday	Sunday
Morning							
Afternoon							
Evening							
Total time (in minutes)							

3 At the end of the week, add up the seven totals. Then divide by seven to find out your average daily exercise time.
Week's total (in minutes) ⬜   Average daily exercise time ⬜

4 How active were you during the week? Did you manage to do 60 minutes of exercise every day? ....
Was your average exercise time more or less than an hour? ....

The brain

The surface of your brain, called the cerebral cortex, is divided into different areas which carry out different tasks. Some areas receive information from your senses. Some trigger body movements, and some are involved in thinking and remembering. Complex brain activities, such as reading, involve several areas working together.

Did you know?

If something makes you feel a strong emotion, such as shock or pleasure, the memory of it is more detailed and easier to remember afterwards.

Memory facts

- You have three types of memories: sensory memories, short-term memories, and long-term memories.
- Information from your sense organs is stored in your sensory memory for just a few seconds.
- If the same information is repeated often, it moves to your long-term memory store.
- Short-term memories fade after a few minutes.
- Long-term memories can last all your life.

Mapping the brain

Read each caption, then number the box beside it to match the correct section of the brain.

[   ] Thoughts happen in the front area of your brain.

[   ] The large area above your brainstem receives and interprets sound signals.

[   ] The area at the back of your brain deals with information from your eyes.

[   ] Sensations such as pain and touch are felt in the area behind the thinking part of your brain.

Cerebrum

2

1

4

3

Front of brain

Brainstem   Cerebellum

Test your memory

1 Look carefully at these 10 objects for 30 seconds.

2 Close the book, wait a minute, then try to write down all the objects you saw.

3 How many of the objects did you remember correctly? [   ]

4 Tomorrow, try again to write a list of the objects, but without opening the book.

5 How many of them did you remember? [   ]

Look on page 44 to find out why you got this result.

Reflexes

A reflex is a body action that happens automatically. Signals pass along neurons and your spinal cord telling part of your body to move, without involving your brain. Some reflexes are actions that happen all the time, such as your heart beat. Other reflexes are sudden emergency actions that protect your body from danger.

How reflexes work

Number the boxes on the diagram to match the stages of how a reflex works.

1. A pain receptor in your hand feels a sharp object.

2. A signal passes along the sensory neurons to your spinal cord.

3. An association neuron in the spinal cord passes the signal to a motor neuron.

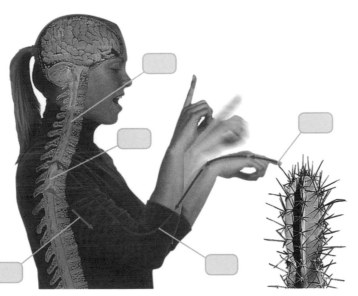

4. The motor neuron carries the signal to a muscle in your upper arm, making it contract so that your hand jerks away.

5. A signal passes to your brain and you feel pain after the reflex has happened.

Test your reflexes

1 Sit in a chair with your legs crossed, so that your lower knee fits into the back of your upper knee.

2 Ask a friend to tap the soft part of your leg just below the kneecap. It may take a bit of practice to tap the right spot.

3 Does your lower leg twitch? ....

4 Try it again. Can you stop your leg twitching by concentrating hard? ....

Look at page 44 to find out why this happens.

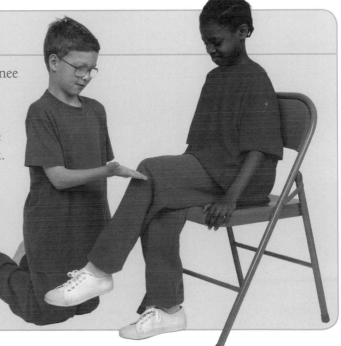

Eyes and seeing

Your eyes are the most complicated sense organs in your body. They collect the light reflected off objects around you, focus it, and transform it into electrical signals to send to your brain. Every second, your brain analyses thousands of signals from your eyes and interprets them as recognizable images.

Did you know?

About 70 per cent of all the sense receptors in your body are found in your eyes.

How your eyes work

Add the words from the list below to complete the captions, using the diagram and the information on page 10 to help you. Choose from:

lens   optic nerve   retina   pupil

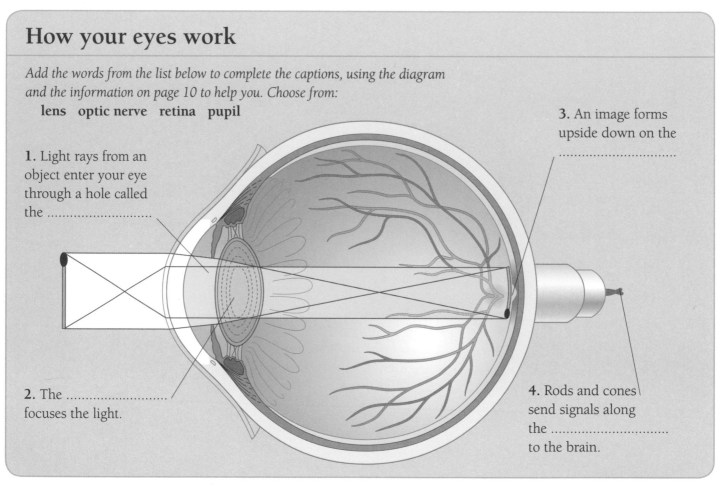

1. Light rays from an object enter your eye through a hole called the ....

2. The .... focuses the light.

3. An image forms upside down on the ....

4. Rods and cones send signals along the .... to the brain.

Letting in the light

In bright light, your pupils constrict (get smaller) to let in less light. In dim light, they dilate (widen) to let in more light. Try this test to see how your pupils change.

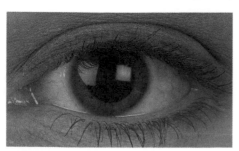

Dilated pupil

1 Put your hand over one eye for 30 seconds, keeping your eye open.

2 Remove your hand, then use a mirror to watch the pupil shrink as it reacts to the light.

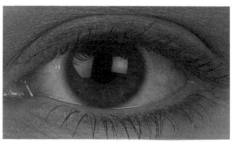

Constricted pupil

Optical illusions

Your brain compares the signals it receives from your eyes with things it has seen in the past, so that it can understand what you are seeing. If your brain receives too little information, or if the information is confusing, it has to guess what you are seeing, and may draw the wrong conclusion. This is called an optical illusion.

Fooling your brain

Look at these strange optical illusions, then turn to page 44 to find out how they work.

1. Stare at this image for a few seconds. Does it look like the pattern is moving?

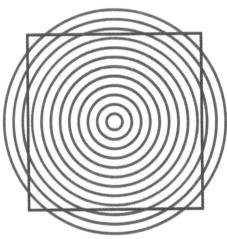

2. Are the blue lines straight or bent? Check with a ruler.

3. Is this a 3-D shape?

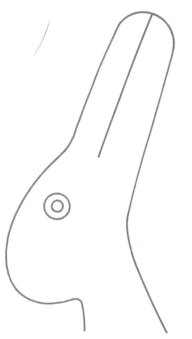

4. Do you see a rabbit or a duck?

Did you know?

If you look closely at an image on the television you will see that it is made up of strips of tiny dots, which glow red, blue, and green. The dots are so tiny and change so fast that your brain interprets them as one clear image.

Using two eyes

Try this experiment to see how your two eyes work together.

1 Roll a sheet of paper into a tube.

2 Using your right hand, hold the tube up to your right eye.

3 Look down the tube, keeping your left eye open.

4 Hold your left hand, with its palm towards you, about two-thirds of the way down the tube, as shown. What do you see?

....

....

Look on page 45 to find out why this happens.

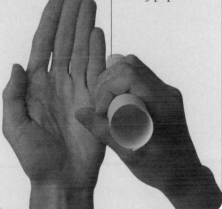

Tube of paper

Ears and hearing

Sound travels in invisible waves through the air. The size of a sound wave is measured in decibels (dB). The quietest sounds a human ear can hear measure about 10 dB, as loud as a person breathing. Sound levels over 100 dB, such as pneumatic drills or loud music, can damage the delicate structures in your ears.

The roar of a jet can reach 120 dB.

How you hear

Add numbers to this diagram to show where each step described below happens. Use the information on page 10 to help you.

1. Sound waves enter the ear through the pinna.

2. Sound waves travel down the ear canal.

3. Sound waves reach the eardrum and make it vibrate.

4. The eardrum passes vibrations to three tiny bones, called ossicles.

5. The sound enters the fluid-filled spiral cochlea.

6. Tiny hairs moving in the cochlea send signals along the auditory nerve to the brain.

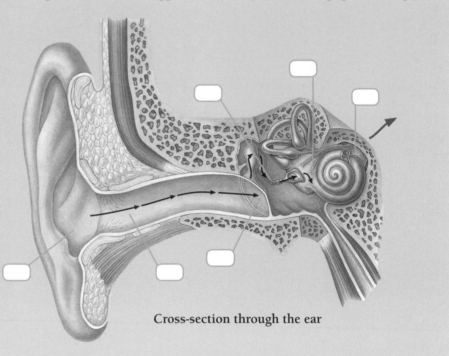

Cross-section through the ear

Balance facts

• Inside your ear, three semicircular canals control your sense of balance.

• These fluid-filled loops are set at right angles to each other.

• As your head moves, fluid inside the semicircular canals moves, disturbing tiny hairs.

• Signals from the hairs tell your brain which way up you are, or which way you are moving.

Feeling dizzy

Try this test to see how fluid moving in your semicircular canals can sometimes make you feel dizzy.

1 Pour a small amount of water into a glass and swirl it round a few times. This represents the fluid moving in your semicircular canals as you spin round.

2 Does the water stop moving straight away when you stop swirling the glass? ....

Look on page 15 to find out why this happens

Semicircular canals and cochlea

Use these picture stickers to complete your Activity pages. Place the gold stars on your Progress chart once you have completed each topic and checked your answers.

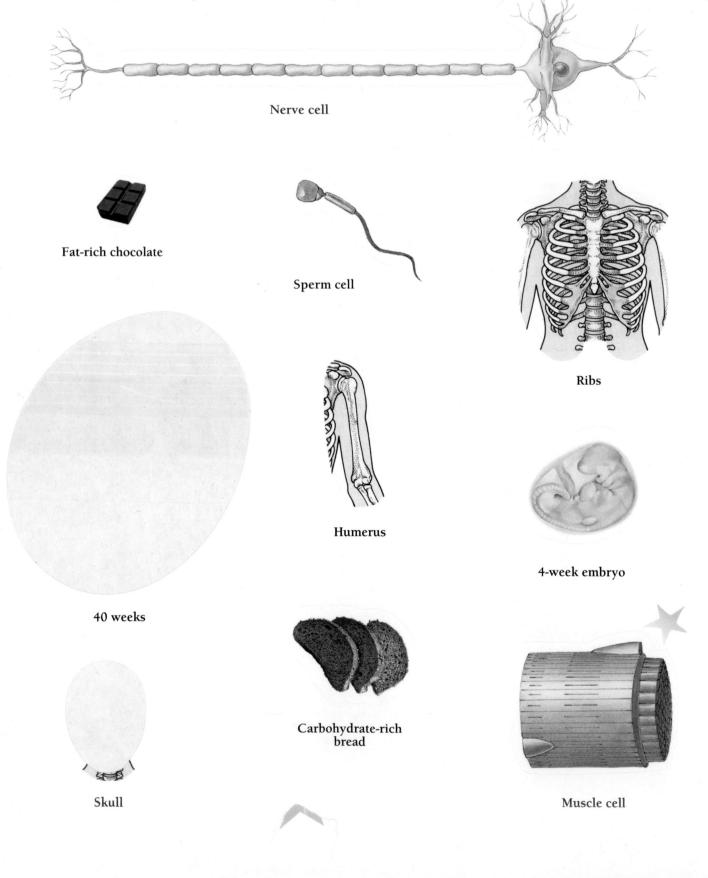

Nerve cell

Fat-rich chocolate

Sperm cell

Ribs

Humerus

4-week embryo

40 weeks

Carbohydrate-rich bread

Skull

Muscle cell

8-week foetus

Tibia and fibula

Red blood cells

Broccoli full of vitamins and minerals

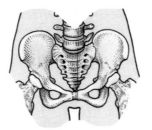

12-week foetus

Protein-rich nuts

24-weeks

Pelvis

Egg cell

Skin and feeling

Your skin is a barrier about 2 mm (less than ¼ in) thick, which covers the outer surface of your body. Skin's main function is to protect your body from bacteria and other harmful substances. Your skin also contains sensory receptors that register heat, cold, pain, and pressure. This allows you to find out about your surroundings. If your skin is injured, it can quickly repair itself.

Skin facts

- The outer layer of skin, the epidermis, contains layers of new and dead skin cells.
- The inner layer, the dermis, is about four times thicker than the epidermis. It is made of living skin cells and contains nerves and blood vessels.
- Beneath your skin is a layer of fat that keeps you warm.
- To cool your body, sweat from sweat glands emerges through pores in the epidermis.
- Each hair on your body has a tiny muscle that makes it stand up when you are cold.

Hot or cold?

Try this test to feel the hot and cold sensors in your skin in action.

1 Fill three glasses with water, one cold, one warm, and one hot (not too hot).

2 Put one finger in the hot glass and one in the cold glass for 30 seconds.

3 Move both fingers into the warm glass.

4 Does the finger from the cold glass feel hot, warm, or cold?

....

5 Does the finger from the hot glass feel hot, warm, or cold?

....

Look at page 45 to find out why this happens.

Cold water   Warm water   Hot water

Did you know?

The human body sheds about 18 kg (40 lb) of dead skin in a lifetime. That's about the weight of a five-year-old child.

Under your skin

Use the information in the fact box above to help you label this diagram with the words in the list below. Choose from:

**epidermis   dermis   nerve ending   blood vessel
fat   sweat gland   pore   muscle   hair**

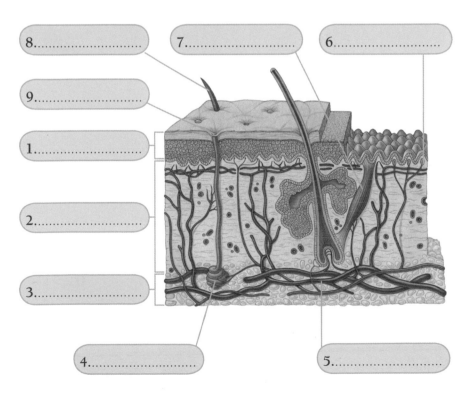

8.........................

7.............................

6.............................

9.........................

1.........................

2.........................

3.........................

4.........................

5.........................

Pumping blood

The body of an average adult contains about 5 litres (9 pints) of blood. That is enough to fill a bucket about half full. The heart pumps all this blood round the body once every minute, working tirelessly throughout a person's life. Over an average lifetime, the heart beats more than three billion times.

Model of outside
of the heart

Heart challenge

Label this diagram using the words in the definition box below, to see how blood flows through your heart. Use the information on this page and on page 11 to help you.

Tip: Remember, you are looking at this heart from the front, so the part you see on the left is actually the right side of the heart, and vice versa.

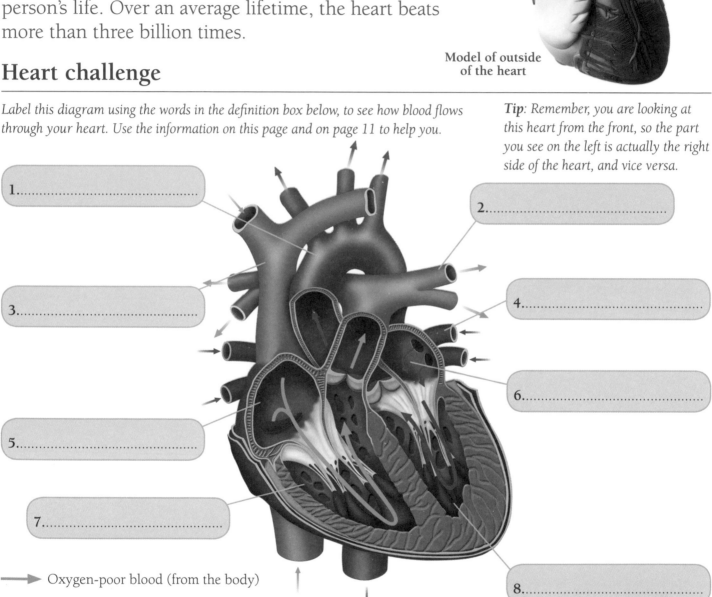

1.....................................

2.....................................

3.....................................

4.....................................

5.....................................

6.....................................

7.....................................

8.....................................

→ Oxygen-poor blood (from the body)

→ Oxygen-rich blood (from the lungs)

Heart definitions

Left or right atrium: one of the two upper chambers of the heart.
Left or right ventricle: one of the two lower chambers of the heart.
Vena cava: blood vessel leading from the body into the heart's right atrium.

Pulmonary veins: blood vessels leading from the lungs to the left atrium.
Pulmonary arteries: blood vessels leading from the heart's right ventricle to the lungs.
Aorta: blood vessel leading from the heart's left ventricle to the rest of the body.

Heart beats

Every beat of your heart sends a high-pressure surge of blood racing into your arteries. You can feel these surges where an artery lies near the surface of your skin. This is known as the pulse. Your heart normally beats about 70 times a minute, but it can rise to 200 when you exercise.

Measure your heart rate

Your pulse rate is the same as your heart rate, so checking your pulse is a good way to find out how hard your heart is working.

1. Use two forefingers to find a pulse on your body. Try inside your wrist or at the side of your throat.

2. Using a stopwatch, count the number of pulses in 10 seconds. Repeat this twice more.
   Result 1 ☐   Result 2 ☐   Result 3 ☐

3. Use a calculator to add your results together, then divide by 3 to get an average.
   Total ☐   Average ☐

4. Multiply the average by 6 to get your rate per minute.
   Resting pulse rate ☐ per minute

5. Now find out your active pulse rate. Run on the spot for a minute, then work out your pulse rate again.
   Result 1 ☐   Result 2 ☐   Result 3 ☐

   Total ☐   Average ☐   Active pulse rate ☐ per minute

6. How much faster was your heart rate after exercising?...

Pulse puzzle

Read this page, then circle the right fact to complete each sentence about your pulse.
1. A pulse can be felt where **an artery** / **a vein** / **a capillary** lies near the skin's surface.
2. An adult's heart normally beats around **100 to 200** / **60 to 80** / **10 to 20** times a minute.
3. When you exercise, your heart rate **lowers** / **stays the same** / **rises**.
4. Your heart rate is **the same** / **different** / **twice as fast** as your pulse rate.

Blood

Arteries carry blood from your heart and have thick walls to withstand high-pressure surges of blood. Veins carry low-pressure blood back to your heart, so they have thinner walls. Tiny blood vessels that carry blood through the tissues have walls just one cell thick.

Vein valves in action

Read the facts about vein valves below, then ask an adult to help you see how they work.

1 Ask an adult to dangle a hand downwards for 30 seconds, so that their veins stand out.

2 Find a section of vein with no branches on the back of their hand. Press your finger on the end of the vein nearest the person's fingers.

3 Place a second finger next to your first finger, then stroke it along the vein towards the wrist. This pushes the blood in the right direction, towards the heart, and empties the vein.

4 Lift your second finger. The vein stays empty, because the valve stops the blood from flowing back. Lift your first finger to see more blood arrive.

Repairing wounds

Number the pictures below in the right order to show how a wound heals.

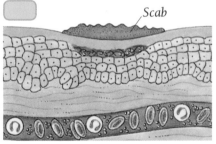
Scab

The clot forms a dry scab, which falls off when the skin below is fully repaired.

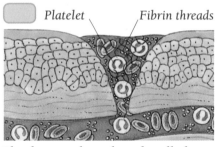
Platelet — Fibrin threads

Platelets produce threads called fibrin, which bind the blood in a clot and stop blood leaking out.

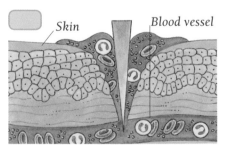
Skin — Blood vessel

An injury to the skin allows blood to start escaping from tiny blood vessels, just below the skin.

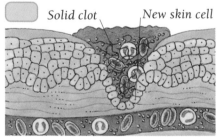
Solid clot — New skin cell

The clot becomes solid. Cells beneath it start to divide, providing new skin cells to repair the injury.

Vein valve facts

- The blood in your veins is under almost no pressure, so your veins contain valves to keep the blood flowing in the right direction.

- Blood flowing the right way (towards the heart) pushes the valve flaps open.

Blood flow — Valve flaps open

Blood flowing the right way

- Blood flowing the wrong way pushes the valve flaps closed.

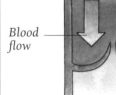
Blood flow — Flaps close to stop blood flowing back.

Blood flowing the wrong way

Breathing

Your body cannot store more than a few minutes' worth of oxygen, so you must continually bring fresh air into your body by breathing. You breathe in and out about 20,000 times a day, but you only notice your breathing if it is disturbed by an irritation, or if you breathe in hard to take in more oxygen when you are exercising.

Breathing puzzle

Write in the correct word to complete these sentences about breathing, using the information on this page to help you. Choose from:

sneezing   yawning   coughing   pant

1. When you are tired, you take more oxygen into your body by ....

2. When mucus or dust irritates the inside of your nose, you blow it out by ....

3. When you've been running fast, you may have to .... to take in enough oxygen.

4. When you have a cold, you remove mucus from your windpipe by ....

Drawing breath

Add arrows to show step by step what happens in your lungs when you breathe. Use the information on page 12 to help you.

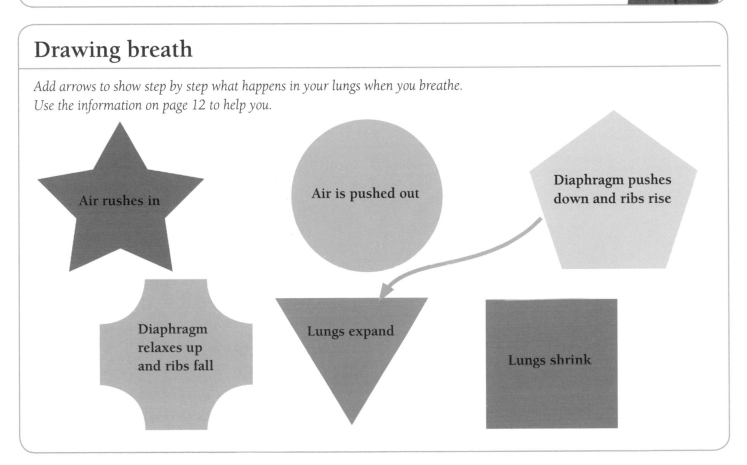

Air rushes in

Air is pushed out

Diaphragm pushes down and ribs rise

Diaphragm relaxes up and ribs fall

Lungs expand

Lungs shrink

A balanced diet

To stay healthy, you should eat a mixture of different types of food, which supply your body with all the nutrients that it needs in order to work properly. You require some nutrients in large quantities and some in much smaller quantities. If you eat the right amounts of all the nutrients regularly, you have a balanced diet.

Food pyramid

This food pyramid shows the proportion of different categories of food you should eat for a healthy, balanced diet. Find the four stickers to add to the right sections on the food pyramid. Then write in the boxes one food from each category that you ate today.

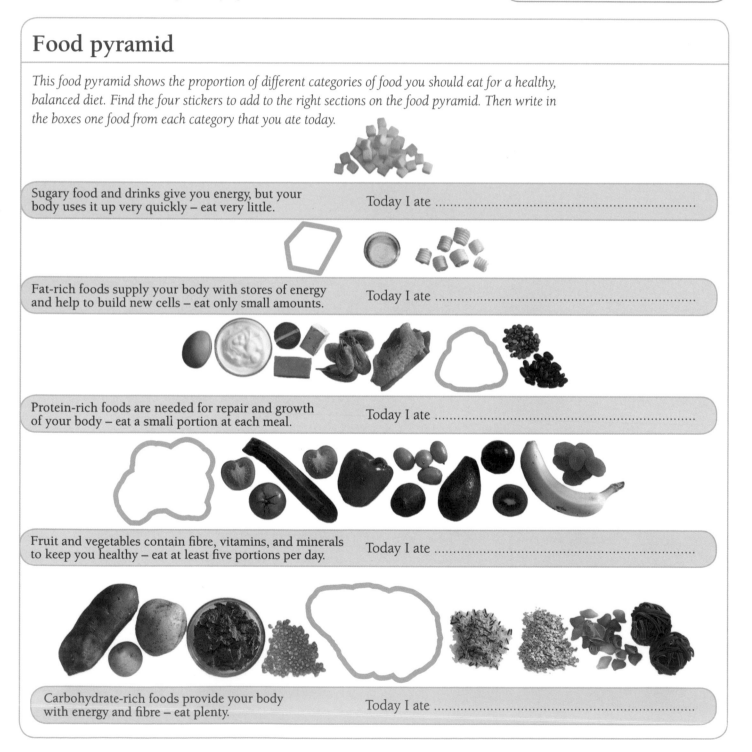

Sugary food and drinks give you energy, but your body uses it up very quickly – eat very little.

Today I ate ....

Fat-rich foods supply your body with stores of energy and help to build new cells – eat only small amounts.

Today I ate ....

Protein-rich foods are needed for repair and growth of your body – eat a small portion at each meal.

Today I ate ....

Fruit and vegetables contain fibre, vitamins, and minerals to keep you healthy – eat at least five portions per day.

Today I ate ....

Carbohydrate-rich foods provide your body with energy and fibre – eat plenty.

Today I ate ....

Taste and smell

Your senses of taste and smell work together to tell you what is good to eat and what might be harmful. On its own, your sense of taste is not very strong. Your brain combines signals from smell receptors and from your eyes to work out what you are tasting.

Tongue map

Different parts of your tongue respond to four different tastes: salty, sweet, sour, and bitter. Draw lines to link each food to the area on the tongue you think would respond to its flavour.

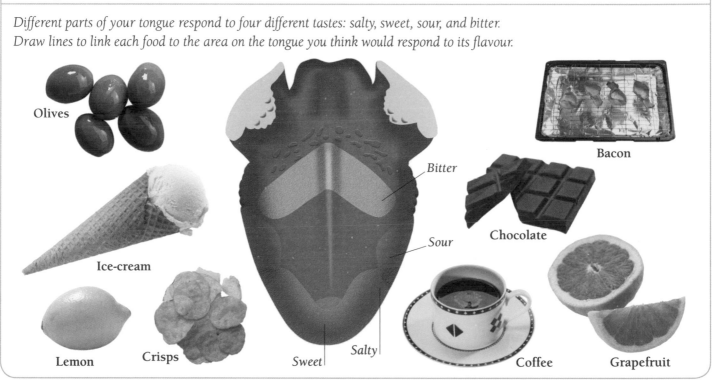

Olives

Bacon

Bitter

Chocolate

Sour

Ice-cream

Lemon

Crisps

Sweet

Salty

Coffee

Grapefruit

Taste test

Find out how smell affects taste with this test. You need:

• *four different foods (such as cheese, chocolate, onion, apple, lemon, or potato) cut into small cubes* • *cocktail sticks* • *a glass of water* • *a blindfold* • *a nose-clip* • *a friend to be the taster*

1 Blindfold the taster and ask him to put on the nose-clip or hold his nose.

2 Pick up a cube of food on a cocktail stick and gently rub it on the taster's tongue for five seconds. Ask him to guess what the food is.

3 Give the taster a drink of water, then repeat the test with each of the other foods. How many did he get right?......................

4 Take off the nose-clip, then ask the taster to taste each of the foods again in the same way. How many did he get right?......................

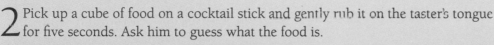

Did your friend get more tastes right with the nose-clip or without?......................

Teeth

When babies are about six months old, teeth start to emerge through their gums. These teeth, called milk teeth, begin to fall out at about five years old, and are replaced by 32 permanent teeth. The front 12 teeth are sharp, for gripping and tearing food. The 20 back teeth are flat, for grinding and crushing food.

Inside a tooth

Number each caption to match the correct part of the tooth.

1
2
3
4
5

☐ The root at the bottom of the tooth attaches it into the gum.

☐ Beneath the enamel, the main part of the tooth is made of dentine.

☐ In the centre of the tooth is the pulp, containing blood vessels and nerves.

☐ The crown is the part of the tooth seen above the gum.

☐ The white outer coating is a hard substance called enamel.

Healthy teeth facts

- Bacteria feed on particles of food left in your mouth.
- Bacteria, food, and saliva form a sticky layer on your teeth called plaque.
- Plaque can make your tooth enamel decay and destroy your teeth.
- Tooth decay can be reduced by brushing twice a day to remove plaque.
- Cutting down on sugary foods and drinks can also help reduce decay, because sugar encourages bacteria to grow.

Did you know?

Some babies are born with a full set of 20 milk teeth.

True or false?

Using the information on this page, tick the boxes to show which of these facts are true and which are false.

	TRUE	FALSE
1. You should cut down on sugar to prevent tooth decay.	☐	☐
2. It's important to brush your teeth more than four times a day.	☐	☐
3. Teeth can be destroyed by dentine.	☐	☐
4. Plaque is a sticky layer that forms on your teeth.	☐	☐

What happens to your food?

Muscle movements push food down your oesophagus to your stomach at a speed of 2.5 to 5 cm (1 to 2 in) per second. Further along your digestive tract, the food moves more slowly to allow nutrients to be absorbed. Food travels through your small intestine at just 1 cm (½ in) per minute.

Muscle movements

Food is pushed through your digestive tract by muscles. To see how this works, you need a small ball to represent the food, and a pair of tights or a long sock to represent your digestive tract.

1 Push the ball into the tights. Make a ring with your fingers next to the ball, as shown in the picture.

2 Squeeze your fingers together, pushing the ball along the tights.

3 Move your fingers next to the ball and squeeze again. Circular muscles along your digestive tract contract in waves, pushing food along in a similar way.

Digestion timetable

Use the information on page 13 to help you add times on this diagram showing how long it can take for food to pass through your digestive system.

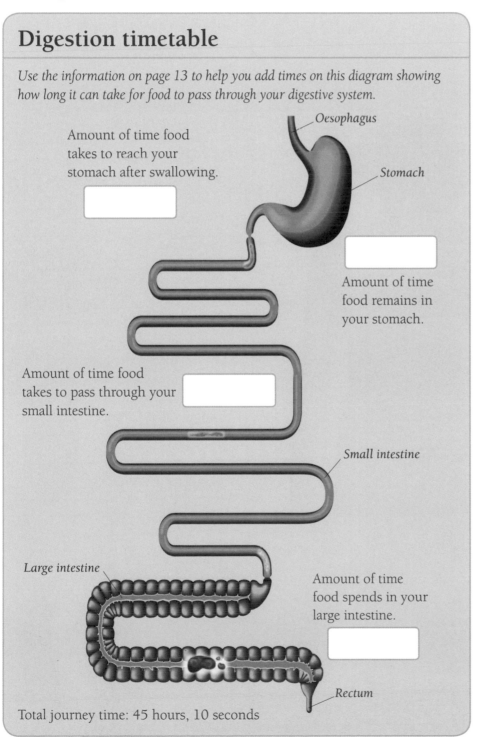

Amount of time food takes to reach your stomach after swallowing.

Oesophagus

Stomach

Amount of time food remains in your stomach.

Amount of time food takes to pass through your small intestine.

Small intestine

Large intestine

Amount of time food spends in your large intestine.

Rectum

Total journey time: 45 hours, 10 seconds

Did you know?

From one end to the other, your digestive tract is about 7 m (24 ft) long.

Waste removal

As your body's systems work, they produce waste products. Waste matter from your digestive system leaves your body as faeces. The waste product of your respiratory system, carbon dioxide, leaves your body as you breathe out. Waste water from all your body processes leaves your body as urine.

Urinary system facts

- Excess water and other waste substances are collected from all the cells in your body by your blood.

- Your two kidneys filter all the blood in your body every five minutes, removing the waste and turning it into urine.

- Urine oozes from each kidney, down a tube called the ureter, and into your bladder.

- Your bladder can contain almost 500 ml (1 pint) of urine. When the bladder is full, urine leaves it through a tube called the urethra.

- An adult's kidneys make approximately 1 litre (2 pints) of urine each day.

Parts of the urinary system

Use the information in the fact box on the right to help you label this diagram with the words in the list. Choose from:

**kidney   bladder
ureter   urethra**

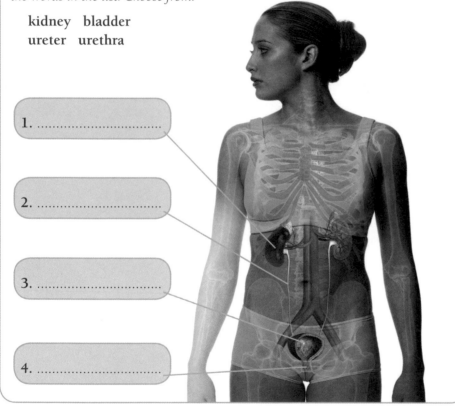

1. ....

2. ....

3. ....

4. ....

Did you know?

Nerves in your bladder wall send signals to your brain when your bladder is full, so that you know you need the toilet. But until the age of about two, the bladder empties automatically – that's why babies need nappies.

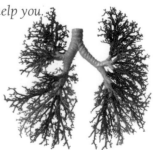

Waste puzzle

Circle the right fact to complete each sentence. Use the information on this page and pages 12–13 to help you.

1. Urine is stored in your **bladder / liver / stomach**.

2. Waste from your digestive system leaves your body as **sweat / faeces / chyme**.

3. The waste product produced by breathing is **air / carbon dioxide / oxygen**.

4. Your kidneys clean your **teeth / bones / blood**.

Bronchioles in the lungs

Chemical messengers

As well as communicating via the nerves of your nervous system, your body uses chemical messengers, called hormones. Hormones travel around your body in your blood. They are produced by special organs, called glands, and by organs such as the pancreas and ovaries. Together, these are called your endocrine system.

Hormones in control

Add the missing words from the list below to complete the captions, using the fact box on the right to help you. Choose from:

adrenal   pancreas   pineal   testes

1. Your .... helps control the amount of sugar in your blood.

2. The .... gland is responsible for regulating your sleep pattern.

3. If something frightens you, your .... gland makes your heart beat faster.

4. Changes to a boy's body at puberty, such as a lower voice, are caused by hormones from his ....

Endocrine facts

- The pineal gland helps to regulate your sleep.
- The pituitary gland controls your growth and the level of water in your body.
- The thyroid gland regulates your body's chemical processes.
- Adrenal glands make your body react fast in emergencies by speeding up your heart rate and breathing.
- The pancreas helps control the level of sugar in your blood.

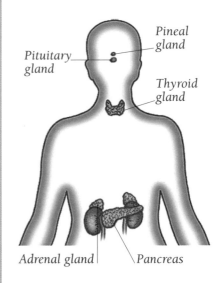

Pineal gland

Pituitary gland

Thyroid gland

Adrenal gland   *Pancreas*

Reproductive glands

- Hormones from a girl's ovaries cause her body development at puberty (from 10 or 11 years).

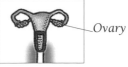

Ovary

- Hormones from the testes cause a boy's body to develop at puberty (from 12 or 13 years).

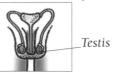

Testis

Making babies

A baby is made from two cells from the reproductive system – an egg cell from a woman and a sperm cell from a man. The sperm joins with the egg in a process called fertilization. Over the next nine months, the fertilized egg develops into a new human being.

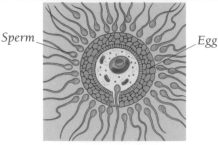

Sperm   *Egg*

Only one sperm will successfully fertilize the egg.

Developing baby

Find the stickers to match the captions about a baby developing in the womb.

1. At 4 weeks, the baby is the size of a pea and it is called an embryo. It has a tail instead of legs and looks like a tadpole.

2. At 8 weeks, the baby is the size of a strawberry and is called a foetus. Its legs and arms are starting to form and it has lost its tail.

3. At 12 weeks, the foetus is about the size of a lemon. It is beginning to look human, though its head is very large.

4. At 24 weeks, the baby is about the size of a melon. Its body has grown into proportion with its head, but it is very thin.

5. At 40 weeks, the baby has grown fatter and rounder and is now ready to be born.

Gene facts

• Each cell in your body carries a set of 46 chromosomes, made from a chemical called DNA.

• Chromosomes contain genes – instructions that tell your body how to grow and function.

• Egg and sperm cells have only 23 chromosomes. When they join to form an embryo, they create a set of 46 chromosomes.

• You inherit half your genes from your mother and half from your father.

• Physical characteristics, such as eye and hair colour, tend to run in families, because they are controlled by genes.

Investigating genes

Read the facts above about genes, then investigate your family members to see how genes have made you alike.

1 Take a good look at your family. Can you see characteristics in yourself and your brothers and sisters that your parents have too? Look at height, eye and hair colour, and the shape of noses and ears.

2 Now look further back in your family tree. Do your grandparents share the same inherited characteristics?

Human life cycle

Like all animals, human beings grow, mature into adults, age, and eventually die. Throughout your life, your body grows and changes, and your mind is developing too. You learn physical skills, from walking to playing sports, and intellectual skills, such as reading, writing, and reasoning. As you age and experience new situations, your emotions develop and mature too.

The human body stops growing at around 20, but continues to change.

How did you grow?

Use photographs to find out how you have changed since you were a baby.

1 Collect some photos of yourself throughout your life and arrange them in order.

3 Which parts of your face and body look the same?

....

....

2 Look at how you have changed physically. Which parts of your face and body look different in photos from the past?

....

....

4 Ask an older relative, such as a parent or grandparent, to show you photos from throughout their life. Put the photos in order and see how the person has changed and how they have stayed the same.

Your family record breakers

Who is the tallest or the oldest in your family? Fill in the chart below with your family record breakers. How does your family compare with the records on the back-cover chart?

RECORD	NAME	STATISTICS
Oldest person		
Youngest person		
Tallest person		
Shortest person		
Person with biggest feet		
Person with longest hair		
Mother with most children		
Oldest married couple		Combined ages:

Cells, tissues, and organs

Tick or number the boxes to answer each question. Check your answers on page 46.

1 Number these body components in order of size, starting with the smallest:

- ☐ **a.** system
- ☐ **b.** tissue
- ☐ **c.** cell
- ☐ **d.** organ

2 How many different types of cell are there in your body?

- ☐ **a.** 2
- ☐ **b.** 20
- ☐ **c.** 200
- ☐ **d.** 2,000

3 Which one of these is *not* part of a cell?

- ☐ **a.** a plasma membrane
- ☐ **b.** a nucleus
- ☐ **c.** cytoplasm
- ☐ **d.** a ligament

4 How are new cells made?

- ☐ **a.** Cells give birth to many baby cells.
- ☐ **b.** New cells are never made.
- ☐ **c.** Cells divide in two.
- ☐ **d.** Cells divide in four.

5 Tissues are made up of:

- ☐ **a.** cells that have the same structure
- ☐ **b.** many different types of cells
- ☐ **c.** two or more types of organ
- ☐ **d.** organs that have the same structure

6 Tick all the types of connective tissue:

- ☐ **a.** fat
- ☐ **b.** blood
- ☐ **c.** muscle
- ☐ **d.** bone

7 Tick all the body organs:

- ☐ **a.** brain
- ☐ **b.** pelvis
- ☐ **c.** liver
- ☐ **d.** skin

8 Several body organs working together to perform a specific job are called:

- ☐ **a.** a tissue
- ☐ **b.** a skeleton
- ☐ **c.** a workforce
- ☐ **d.** a system

9 Which of these is *not* a body system?

- ☐ **a.** digestive
- ☐ **b.** epithelial
- ☐ **c.** skeletal
- ☐ **d.** muscular

10 The function of your circulatory system is:

- ☐ **a.** removing waste from your body
- ☐ **b.** moving blood around your body
- ☐ **c.** processing food
- ☐ **d.** moving your body

11 Which of these organs forms part of your respiratory system?

- ☐ **a.** your liver
- ☐ **b.** your brain
- ☐ **c.** your stomach
- ☐ **d.** your lungs

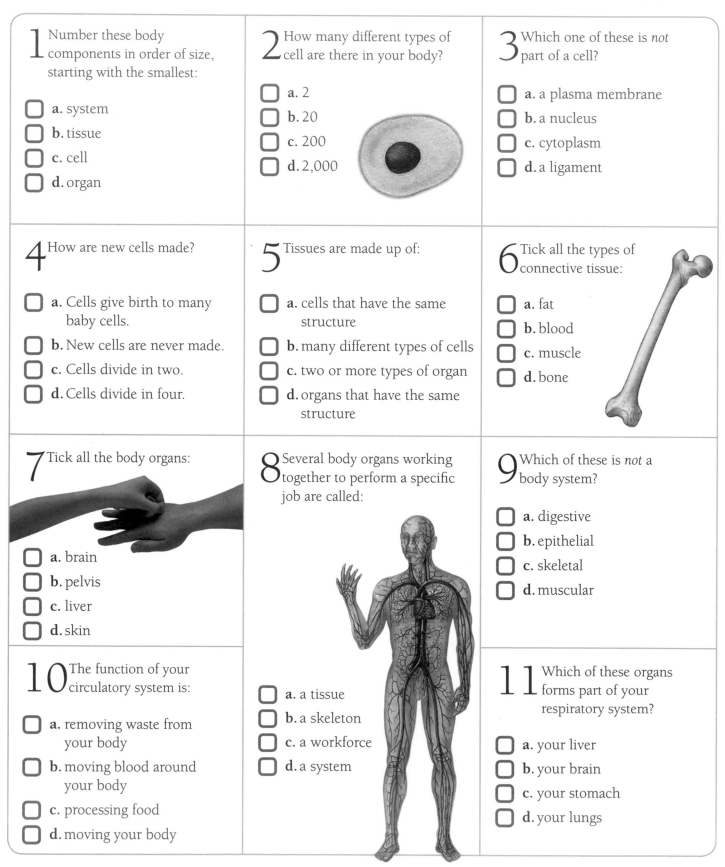

Bones, muscles, and exercise

Tick or number the boxes to answer each question. Check your answers on page 46.

1 How many bones are there in an adult's body?

☐ **a.** 3,024
☐ **b.** 2,006
☐ **c.** 300
☐ **d.** 206

2 Which of these is *not* a bone?

☐ **a.** the fibula
☐ **b.** the pelvis
☐ **c.** the radius
☐ **d.** the biceps

3 The bony structure that runs down your back is called your:

☐ **a.** skull
☐ **b.** spine
☐ **c.** femur
☐ **d.** funny bone

4 What type of joint is this?

☐ **a.** a pivot joint
☐ **b.** a hinge joint
☐ **c.** a ball and socket joint
☐ **d.** an ellipsoidal joint

5 The bands of tissue that hold your joints together are called:

☐ **a.** ligaments
☐ **b.** cartilage
☐ **c.** tendons
☐ **d.** skin

6 Which of these is *not* a type of muscle:

☐ **a.** smooth
☐ **b.** rough
☐ **c.** skeletal
☐ **d.** cardiac

7 What do muscles need in order to work?

☐ **a.** water
☐ **b.** heat
☐ **c.** carbon dioxide
☐ **d.** oxygen

8 When a muscle contracts:

☐ **a.** it pushes the bones it is attached to
☐ **b.** it pulls the bones it is attached to
☐ **c.** it bends the bones it is attached to

9 Tick all the things you should do to keep your body fit and healthy:

☐ **a.** read at least one book every week
☐ **b.** clean your teeth twice a day
☐ **c.** eat a balanced diet
☐ **d.** take regular exercise
☐ **e.** never go outside when it is cold

10 How much exercise do experts say children should take every day?

☐ **a.** 30 minutes
☐ **b.** 60 minutes
☐ **c.** 90 minutes
☐ **d.** 120 minutes

Heart, blood, and lungs

Tick or number the boxes to answer each question. Check your answers on page 46.

1 What substance does blood pick up in your lungs?

- ☐ **a.** water
- ☐ **b.** red blood cells
- ☐ **c.** oxygen
- ☐ **d.** carbon dioxide

2 Your heart is about the same size as:

- ☐ **a.** your big toe
- ☐ **b.** your fist
- ☐ **c.** a bucket
- ☐ **d.** a football

3 Tick all the items you would find in your heart:

- ☐ **a.** a diaphragm
- ☐ **b.** a ventricle
- ☐ **c.** an atrium
- ☐ **d.** a cochlea

4 Your pulse is:

- ☐ **a.** a high-pressure surge of blood flowing through your veins
- ☐ **b.** a high-pressure surge of blood flowing through your arteries
- ☐ **c.** an automatic movement of your diaphragm
- ☐ **d.** part of a vein that stops blood flowing backwards

5 How much blood does an adult's body contain?

- ☐ **a.** 1.25 litres (2¼ pints)
- ☐ **b.** 2.5 litres (4½ pints)
- ☐ **c.** 5 litres (9 pints)
- ☐ **d.** 10 litres (18 pints)

6 Which of these is *not* a component of blood?

- ☐ **a.** white blood cells
- ☐ **b.** red blood cells
- ☐ **c.** blue blood cells
- ☐ **d.** plasma
- ☐ **e.** platelets

7 Tick all the items that are part of your respiratory system:

- ☐ **a.** sclera
- ☐ **b.** bronchus
- ☐ **c.** lungs
- ☐ **d.** trachea

8 Number this sequence to show what happens after you breathe air into your lungs:

- ☐ **a.** Oxygen-poor blood flows back to your heart.
- ☐ **b.** Oxygen-rich blood from your lungs flows to your heart and is pumped around your body.
- ☐ **c.** Oxygen from the air in your lungs passes into your blood.
- ☐ **d.** Your heart pumps oxygen-poor blood back to your lungs.
- ☐ **e.** Your body tissues use up the oxygen from your blood.

9 The tiny air sacs in your lungs are called:

- ☐ **a.** alveoli
- ☐ **b.** arteries
- ☐ **c.** lobes
- ☐ **d.** ribs

10 You sneeze when:

- ☐ **a.** you need to get rid of dust in your windpipe
- ☐ **b.** dust irritates the inside of your nose
- ☐ **c.** you've been running fast
- ☐ **d.** you are feeling tired

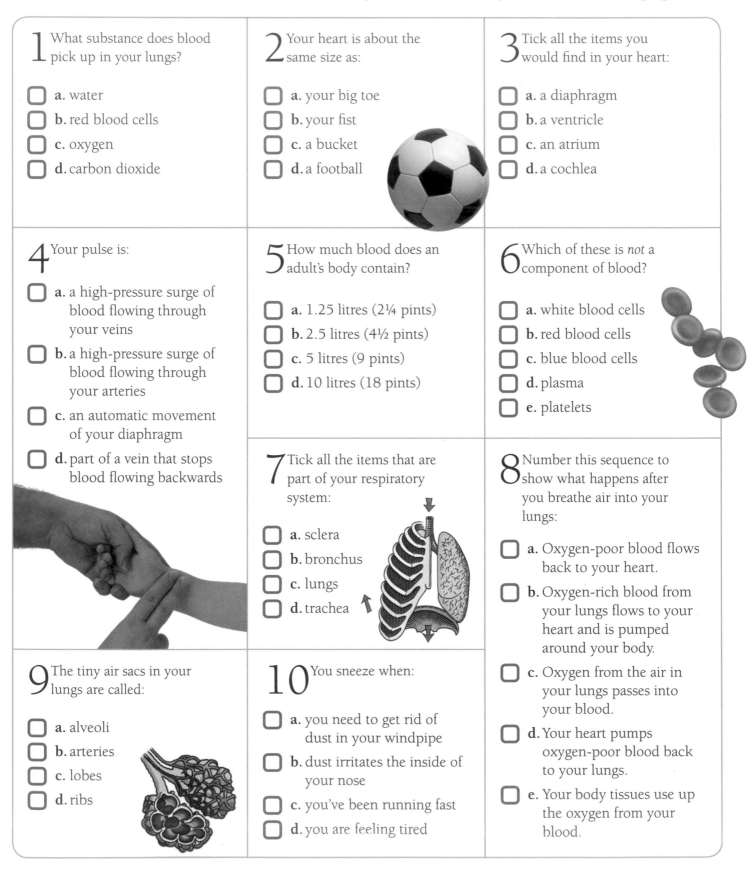

Stomach, intestines, and diet

Tick or number the boxes to answer each question. Check your answers on page 46.

1 The tube that runs from your mouth to your stomach is called the:

- ☐ **a.** vena cava
- ☐ **b.** trachea
- ☐ **c.** ventricle
- ☐ **d.** oesophagus

2 Number these organs to show the order that food passes through them as it travels along your digestive tract:

- ☐ **a.** large intestine
- ☐ **b.** oesophagus
- ☐ **c.** small intestine
- ☐ **d.** stomach

3 What pushes food through your digestive tract?

- ☐ **a.** gravity
- ☐ **b.** muscle movements
- ☐ **c.** your heart
- ☐ **d.** breathing

4 How long does it usually take for a meal to pass all the way through your digestive tract?

- ☐ **a.** up to 45 minutes
- ☐ **b.** about six hours
- ☐ **c.** up to 46 hours
- ☐ **d.** more than two days

5 What is absorbed through the walls of your large intestine?

- ☐ **a.** fibre
- ☐ **b.** water
- ☐ **c.** blood
- ☐ **d.** faeces

6 How long is your small intestine?

- ☐ **a.** 30 cm (1 ft)
- ☐ **b.** 1.5 m (5 ft)
- ☐ **c.** 5 m (17 ft)
- ☐ **d.** 20 m (60 ft)

7 Which of these foods does *not* contain protein:

- ☐ **a.** eggs
- ☐ **b.** ham
- ☐ **c.** oranges
- ☐ **d.** yoghurt

8 Tick two types of food you should eat plenty of every day:

- ☐ **a.** carbohydrate-rich foods, such as bread and pasta
- ☐ **b.** crisps
- ☐ **c.** fruit and vegetables
- ☐ **d.** sugary foods and drinks

9 You produce urine in your:

- ☐ **a.** bladder
- ☐ **b.** kidneys
- ☐ **c.** large intestine
- ☐ **d.** stomach

10 Tick the thing that is *not* a body waste product:

- ☐ **a.** urine
- ☐ **b.** faeces
- ☐ **c.** chyme
- ☐ **d.** carbon dioxide

11 How many teeth does an adult have?

- ☐ **a.** 32
- ☐ **b.** 20
- ☐ **c.** 144
- ☐ **d.** 40

Brain, nerves, and senses

Tick or number the boxes to answer each question. Check your answers on page 46.

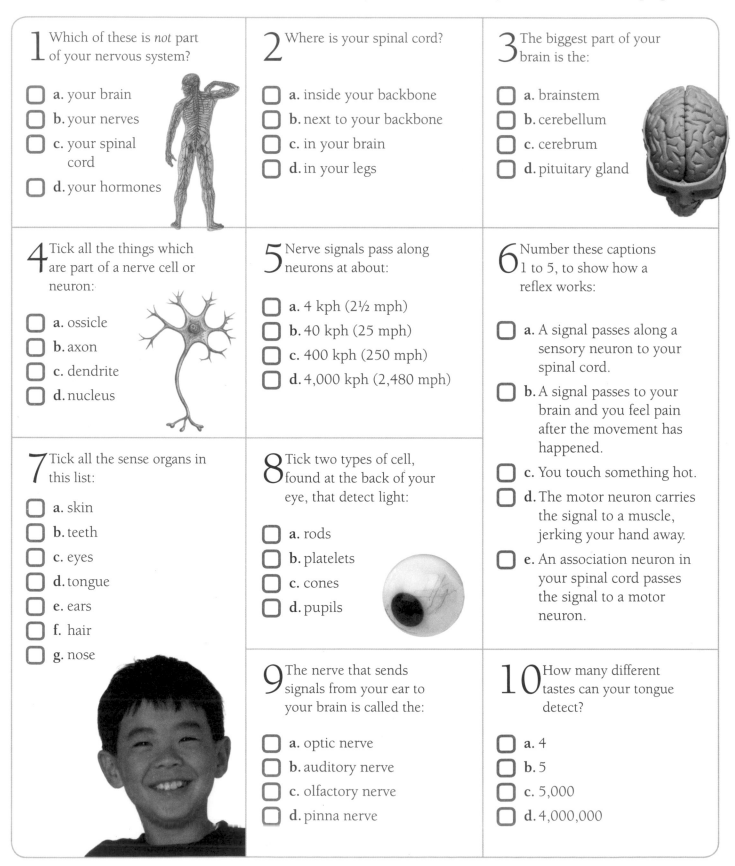

1 Which of these is *not* part of your nervous system?

- ☐ **a.** your brain
- ☐ **b.** your nerves
- ☐ **c.** your spinal cord
- ☐ **d.** your hormones

2 Where is your spinal cord?

- ☐ **a.** inside your backbone
- ☐ **b.** next to your backbone
- ☐ **c.** in your brain
- ☐ **d.** in your legs

3 The biggest part of your brain is the:

- ☐ **a.** brainstem
- ☐ **b.** cerebellum
- ☐ **c.** cerebrum
- ☐ **d.** pituitary gland

4 Tick all the things which are part of a nerve cell or neuron:

- ☐ **a.** ossicle
- ☐ **b.** axon
- ☐ **c.** dendrite
- ☐ **d.** nucleus

5 Nerve signals pass along neurons at about:

- ☐ **a.** 4 kph (2½ mph)
- ☐ **b.** 40 kph (25 mph)
- ☐ **c.** 400 kph (250 mph)
- ☐ **d.** 4,000 kph (2,480 mph)

6 Number these captions 1 to 5, to show how a reflex works:

- ☐ **a.** A signal passes along a sensory neuron to your spinal cord.
- ☐ **b.** A signal passes to your brain and you feel pain after the movement has happened.
- ☐ **c.** You touch something hot.
- ☐ **d.** The motor neuron carries the signal to a muscle, jerking your hand away.
- ☐ **e.** An association neuron in your spinal cord passes the signal to a motor neuron.

7 Tick all the sense organs in this list:

- ☐ **a.** skin
- ☐ **b.** teeth
- ☐ **c.** eyes
- ☐ **d.** tongue
- ☐ **e.** ears
- ☐ **f.** hair
- ☐ **g.** nose

8 Tick two types of cell, found at the back of your eye, that detect light:

- ☐ **a.** rods
- ☐ **b.** platelets
- ☐ **c.** cones
- ☐ **d.** pupils

9 The nerve that sends signals from your ear to your brain is called the:

- ☐ **a.** optic nerve
- ☐ **b.** auditory nerve
- ☐ **c.** olfactory nerve
- ☐ **d.** pinna nerve

10 How many different tastes can your tongue detect?

- ☐ **a.** 4
- ☐ **b.** 5
- ☐ **c.** 5,000
- ☐ **d.** 4,000,000

Hormones and growth

Tick or number the boxes to answer each question. Check your answers on page 46.

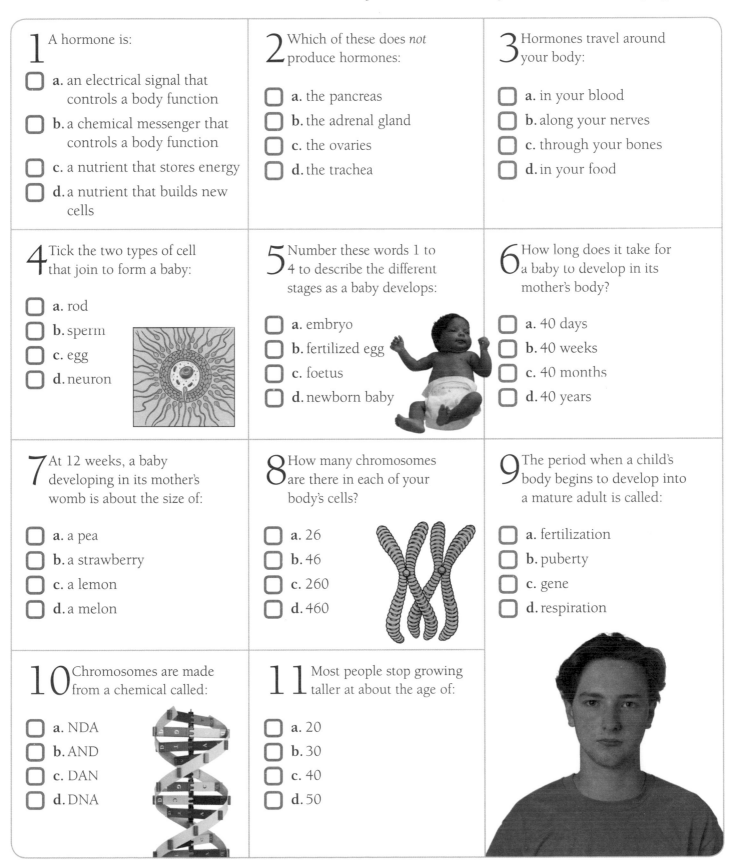

1 A hormone is:

☐ **a.** an electrical signal that controls a body function

☐ **b.** a chemical messenger that controls a body function

☐ **c.** a nutrient that stores energy

☐ **d.** a nutrient that builds new cells

2 Which of these does *not* produce hormones:

☐ **a.** the pancreas

☐ **b.** the adrenal gland

☐ **c.** the ovaries

☐ **d.** the trachea

3 Hormones travel around your body:

☐ **a.** in your blood

☐ **b.** along your nerves

☐ **c.** through your bones

☐ **d.** in your food

4 Tick the two types of cell that join to form a baby:

☐ **a.** rod

☐ **b.** sperm

☐ **c.** egg

☐ **d.** neuron

5 Number these words 1 to 4 to describe the different stages as a baby develops:

☐ **a.** embryo

☐ **b.** fertilized egg

☐ **c.** foetus

☐ **d.** newborn baby

6 How long does it take for a baby to develop in its mother's body?

☐ **a.** 40 days

☐ **b.** 40 weeks

☐ **c.** 40 months

☐ **d.** 40 years

7 At 12 weeks, a baby developing in its mother's womb is about the size of:

☐ **a.** a pea

☐ **b.** a strawberry

☐ **c.** a lemon

☐ **d.** a melon

8 How many chromosomes are there in each of your body's cells?

☐ **a.** 26

☐ **b.** 46

☐ **c.** 260

☐ **d.** 460

9 The period when a child's body begins to develop into a mature adult is called:

☐ **a.** fertilization

☐ **b.** puberty

☐ **c.** gene

☐ **d.** respiration

10 Chromosomes are made from a chemical called:

☐ **a.** NDA

☐ **b.** AND

☐ **c.** DAN

☐ **d.** DNA

11 Most people stop growing taller at about the age of:

☐ **a.** 20

☐ **b.** 30

☐ **c.** 40

☐ **d.** 50

Activity answers

Once you have completed each page of activities, check your answers below:

Page 14 Cells and tissues puzzle
1 just one type
2 200
3 sperm
4 two or more types

Page 15 Guess the system
1 respiratory
2 digestive
3 muscular
4 circulatory
5 skeletal
6 nervous

Page 16 Skeleton jigsaw

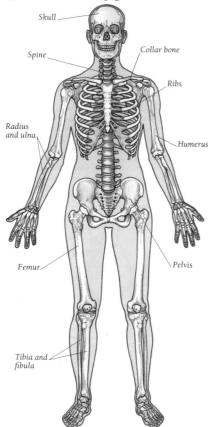

Skull
Spine
Collar bone
Ribs
Radius and ulna
Humerus
Femur
Pelvis
Tibia and fibula

Page 16 Sorting bones
1 femur (leg bone)
2 calcineus (heel bone)
3 parietal (skull bone)
4 sphenoid (bone from inside skull)
5 patella (kneecap)

Page 17 Joint puzzle
1 ball and socket / shoulder
2 ellipsoidal / wrist
3 hinge / knee
4 head / pivot

Page 17 True or false?
1 True
2 True
3 True
4 False – The skeleton stops growing by the age of about 18 years.

Page 18 Muscle types
1 cardiac
2 skeletal
3 smooth

Page 18 Clench test
You should manage more clenches with your hand held by your side. Blood flows more quickly downwards than upwards, so the blood provides the muscles in your lowered hand with oxygen more quickly than the muscles in your raised hand. With more oxygen, the muscles of your lowered hand do not tire so easily.

Page 18 Relax test
Your fingers should move towards each other as they relax. When they are not active, skeletal muscles return to a relaxed position, which they can maintain with only a little energy.

Page 20 Mapping the brain
1 Thoughts happen in the front area of your brain.
2 Sensations such as pain and touch are felt in the area behind the thinking part of your brain.
3 The large area above your brainstem receives and interprets sound signals.

4 The area at the back of your brain deals with information from your eyes.

Page 20 Test your memory
You probably remembered fewer objects the second day, because the 10 objects were only stored in your short-term memory.

Page 21 How reflexes work

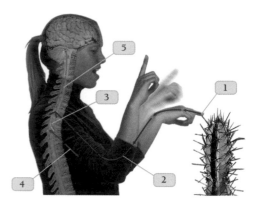

Page 21 Test your reflexes
Receptors below your knee interpret this tap as your knee being overstretched. They signal to a thigh muscle, telling it to tighten in order to straighten your knee. You cannot stop your leg moving, because this action is a reflex not consciously controlled by your brain.

Page 22 How your eyes work
1 pupil
2 lens
3 retina
4 optic nerve

Page 23 Fooling your brain
1 The lines and spaces in this picture are so close together that your eyes scan them in rapid jerks, which gives your brain the impression that the lines are moving.
2 The unusual combination of shapes made by the square lines on the circles confuses your brain, so it sees the blue lines as bent.

3 This shape confuses your brain's mechanism for seeing in three dimensions. Your brain recognizes the shading of this shape as showing a 3-D shape, but can also see that it could never exist in real life.

4 Your brain interprets this as either a rabbit or a duck, but can't see both pictures at once, so it switches from one to the other.

Page 23 Using two eyes

You should see a hole through your hand. Each of your eyes sees a slightly different view of whatever you are looking at. Your brain adds these two images together to make one image. Usually this works, as the two viewpoints overlap in the middle. With one eye shielded from the other, the two viewpoints are different in the middle, leading to this very strange result.

Page 24 How you hear

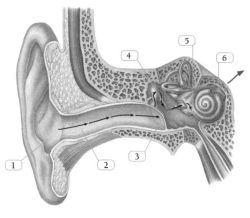

Page 24 Feeling dizzy

The liquid in the glass keeps on swirling after the glass stops moving. The same thing happens if you spin around and suddenly stop. The liquid in your semicircular canals keeps moving, so your brain thinks you are still moving. But your eyes tell your brain that you are not moving. These confused messages make you feel dizzy.

Page 25 Hot or cold?

4 Hot
5 Cold

Your temperature sensors respond to changes in temperature. So when you move the finger from cold water into warm water, sensors detect an increase in heat and the water feels hot. Sensors in the finger from the hot water detect an increase in coldness, so the water feels cold.

Page 25 Under your skin

1 epidermis
2 dermis
3 fat
4 sweat gland
5 blood vessel
6 nerve ending
7 muscle
8 hair
9 pore

Page 26 Heart challenge

1 aorta
2 pulmonary artery
3 vena cava
4 pulmonary vein
5 right atrium
6 left atrium
7 right ventricle
8 left ventricle

Page 27 Pulse puzzle

1 an artery
2 60 to 80
3 rises
4 same

Page 28 Repairing wounds

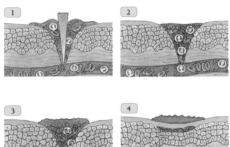

Page 29 Breathing puzzle

1 yawning
2 sneezing
3 pant
4 coughing

Page 29 Drawing breath

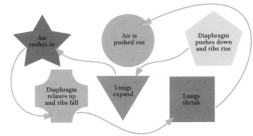

Page 31 Tongue map

Salty: crisps, bacon
Sweet: chocolate, ice-cream
Sour: grapefruit, lemon
Bitter: coffee, olives

These are the most usual answers, but people's sense of taste varies, so you might have different ideas, or think that a food contains more than one of these flavours.

Page 31 Taste test

The taster should identify more foods correctly without the nose clip. Wearing the nose clip, the taster can only use their sense of taste, which is not very strong. Without the nose clip, the taster can use their sense of smell too, making it much easier to taste and identify the foods.

Page 32 Inside a tooth

1 The crown is the part of the tooth seen above the gum.
2 The white outer coating is a hard substance called enamel.
3 Beneath the enamel the main part of the tooth is made from dentine.
4 In the centre of the tooth is the pulp, containing blood vessels and nerves.
5 The root at the bottom of the tooth attaches it to the gum.

Page 32 True or false?
1 True
2 False – You should brush your teeth twice a day.
3 False – Teeth can be destroyed by plaque. Dentine is a substance that forms part of your teeth.
4 True

Page 33 Digestion timetable
10 seconds: Amount of time food takes to reach your stomach after swallowing
4 hours: Amount of time food remains in your stomach
5 hours: Amount of time food takes to pass through your small intestine
36 hours: Amount of time food spends in your large intestine

Page 34 Parts of the urinary system
1 kidney
2 ureter
3 bladder
4 urethra

Page 34 Waste puzzle
1 bladder
2 faeces
3 carbon dioxide
4 blood

Page 35 Hormones in control
1 pancreas
2 pineal
3 adrenal
4 testes

Quick quiz answers

Once you have completed each page of quiz questions, check your answers below.

Page 38
Cells, tissues, and organs
1 a4, b2, c1, d3 2 c 3 d 4 c 5 a
6 a, b, d 7 a, c, d 8 d 9 b 10 b
11 d

Page 39
Bones, muscles, and exercise
1 d 2 d 3 b 4 c 5 a 6 b 7 d 8 b
9 b, c, d 10 b

Page 40
Heart, blood, and lungs
1 c 2 b 3 b, c 4 b 5 c 6 c 7 b, c, d
8 a4, b2, c1, d 5, e 3 9 a 10 b

Page 41
Stomach, intestines, and diet
1 d 2 a4, b1, c3, d2 3 b 4 c 5 b 6 c
7 c 8 a, c 9 b 10 c 11 a

Page 42
Brain, nerves, and senses
1 d 2 a 3 c 4 b, c, d 5 c
6 a2, b5, c1, d4, e3 7 a, c, d, e, g
8 a, c 9 b 10 a

Page 43
Hormones and growth
1 b 2 d 3 a 4 b, c 5 a2, b1, c3, d4
6 b 7 c 8 b 9 b 10 d 11 a

Acknowledgements

The publisher would like to thank Alyson Silverwood for proof-reading.

The publisher would like to thank the following for their kind permission to reproduce their photographs:

(Key: a-above; b-below/bottom; c-centre; l-left; r-right; t-top)

DK Images: Denoyer-Geppert International 26tr; ESPL / Denoyer-Geppert International 42tr; The Science Museum, London 43bl; Spike Walker (Microworld Services) 14tr.

Jacket images: Front: **DK Images:** Natural History Museum, London r.

All other images © Dorling Kindersley For further information see: www.dkimages.com

PROGRESS CHART

Chart your progress as you work through the activity and quiz pages in this book.
First check your answers, then stick a gold star in the correct box below.

Page	Topic	Star	Page	Topic	Star	Page	Topic	Star
14	Body building blocks	⭐	24	Ears and hearing	⭐	34	Waste removal	⭐
15	Body systems	⭐	25	Skin and feeling	⭐	35	Chemical messengers	⭐
16	Big bones, small bones	⭐	26	Pumping blood	⭐	36	Making babies	⭐
17	Big bones, small bones	⭐	27	Heart beats	⭐	37	Human life cycle	⭐
18	Moving muscles	⭐	28	Blood	⭐	38	Cells, tissues, and organs	⭐
19	Fit and healthy	⭐	29	Breathing	⭐	39	Bones, muscles, and exercise	⭐
20	The brain	⭐	30	A balanced diet	⭐	40	Heart, blood, and lungs	⭐
21	Reflexes	⭐	31	Taste and smell	⭐	41	Stomach, intestines, and diet	⭐
22	Eyes and seeing	⭐	32	Teeth	⭐	42	Brain, nerves, and senses	⭐
23	Optical illusions	⭐	33	What happens to your food?	⭐	43	Hormones and growth	⭐

EYEWITNESS PROJECT BOOKS
HUMAN BODY

★ ★ ★ ★ ★ ★ ★ ★

CERTIFICATE OF EXCELLENCE

Congratulations to

(Name) . . . .

for successfully completing this book on

(Award date) . . . .